Starting a Small
Restaurant

Starting a Small
Restaurant

❖ ❖ ❖

How to Make Your Dream a Reality

All-New Revised Edition

Daniel Miller

The Harvard Common Press

Boston, Massachusetts

The Harvard Common Press
535 Albany Street
Boston, Massachusetts 02118
www.harvardcommonpress.com

Printed in the United States of America
Printed on acid-free paper

Library of Congress Cataloging-in-Publication Data

Miller, Daniel, 1932–
    Starting a small restaurant : how to make your dream a reality /
Daniel Miller.—Rev. ed.
        p.   cm.
    Includes index.
    ISBN 1-55832-286-8 (hardcover : alk. paper)—ISBN 1-55832-287-6
(pbk. : alk. paper)
    1. Restaurant management.   I. Title.
    TX911.3.M27M54 2006
    647.95'068—dc22

                                                    2005020980

ISBN-13: 978-1-55832-286-8 (hardcover); 978-1-55832-287-5 (paperback)
ISBN-10: 1-55832-286-8 (hardcover); 1-55832-287-6 (paperback)

Special bulk-order discounts are available on this and other Harvard
Common Press books. Companies and organizations may purchase books
for premiums or resale, or may arrange a custom edition, by contacting
the Marketing Director at the address above.

Cover design by Night & Day Design
Interior design by rlf design

10 9 8 7 6 5 4 3 2

To Shirley,

who has something special

from start to finish

Contents

Acknowledgments

This book could never have been if not for Shirley; Hilda Steele; Sheree; Abe and Ruth; Becky, Scott, and Mike; Andy and Jack Herrington; Jim Harris; Ken Kelly; Del Stanton; David Megibow; Brian and Sylvia Hume; Mabel Souza; Warren Leopold; Karen Gunther Theisz; Wilfred Lyons; Paul and Louise Squibb; Bob Doerr; Warren Talcott; Robert May, R.N.; Leslie; Ed and Kathleen; the 1971 San Fernando earthquake; Cambria, California, and a cast of thousands. But they didn't write it.

Also, additional thanks go to Jim and Karen Clarke, Joanne and Ross Currie, Eduardo Faubert, Edward Miller and Teresa Parker, Scott Miller, Eve and Tom Neuhaus, Keith Pellemeier, and Barbara Rubin for their warm hospitality, inspiration, and willingness to share their knowledge and experiences.

Finally, this revision reflects the editorial acumen of Pam Hoenig. Her improvements to the way I have expressed my ideas are invaluable, and for that I am very grateful.

Introduction

Have you tried a local, family-run restaurant recently? If you enjoyed it, compare it with what is described in this book. But if you found the place unsatisfactory, perhaps you can discover in these pages examples of what should have been done. If so, I urge you to strike a blow for restaurant customers everywhere by returning to the place to give it another chance. Take this book with you. If the restaurant has not improved, leave the book with the owner when you send back your uneaten meal. Then go home, instead of to another restaurant. Have a glass of wine and relax, and you'll feel better about the experience. Then resolve to open your own restaurant—or to buy the place you just visited and improve it.

I have a theory about small restaurants and their unique role in today's stressful American society. They provide the public with one of the last vestiges of true enterprise and inventiveness in the current economic corporate concentration camp mentality. A small restaurant is one of the few places where the distraught parents of small children can regain their sanity and feelings of romance, where the weary traveler can feel truly at home, where a family can enjoy each other's company but not have to do the dishes, and where the owner's hard work and love of excellence show. Once the public discovers one of these good small restaurants, it really is appreciative and supportive. The place may eventually change, expand beyond control, go out of business, or fail to maintain quality—but the customer always retains the choice of whether to patronize it. What matters in the long run is that such places can continue to spring up, like good mushrooms.

This book is for anyone who has thought about opening a small restaurant, or who has a friend who wants to do so. It is my purpose here to try to make it a little less scary for people without professional restaurant experience to be good mushrooms. Like the lowly mushroom, the small restaurant, if prepared properly, can overcome even an inauspicious beginning and add a unique and distinctive flavor to life.

Introduction to the New Edition

My experiences as a founder of the Grey Fox Inn, a small restaurant in Cambria, California, were instrumental in the creation of this book. At the time of the restaurant's founding, in the mid 1970s, no such book existed. My co-founders and I learned everything we needed to know about dining room practice, establishing relationships with suppliers, and other important aspects of the restaurant business through the guidance of a few experienced local workers and advisors. Everyone involved in the business has a stake in the success of a small fine restaurant, so they are generous with their help and advice.

The Grey Fox Inn's success rested primarily on the genius of one of the owners, who was also the chef. Her sense of style and personality infused every aspect of the operation. The relationships described in this book were experienced in real life and benefited from the loyalty and respect that the entire staff bore for the chef. Although the Grey Fox Inn no longer exists, the building it occupied remains in use to this day as a highly popular restaurant venue.

In the three decades since I first wrote this book, Americans have learned much about what is good to eat and where to find it. You are probably someone who appreciates locally baked bread and rolls and freshly prepared vegetables, fruit, fish, and fowl, combined stylishly for a meal. You may also want your meat to be raised humanely without harmful substances. By attending one of the many culinary arts training academies now operating, you may have prepared for a career in food service. Thirty years ago, an amateur without formal training stood a fair chance of success. My objective then was to encourage those with the requisite artistry and culinary sense to fulfill their dreams. This edition recognizes that if you have more formal training, in both food selection and preparation, as well as in business operations, you will have a greater chance for success than the amateur cook. I believe that today's sophisticated diners and the demands of seven days per week operation require that aspiring restaurateurs obtain formal training to ensure consistent quality. The enduring aim of this book is to encourage you to focus your talents and sensibilities toward owning and successfully operating a smaller restaurant rather than one run by a large corporate chain.

Fortunately, much has remained unchanged in the intervening years. Those values I praised in the original Introduction remain foremost in the smaller food service establishment, whether run by a family or partners. Although there has been a proliferation of restaurants of all sorts, the increase has resulted from a major shift in the typical workday and spending choices of patrons. People appreciate better, fresher food, but they have less time to prepare it at home. The stress in American family life, especially for those who work in the corporate business world, has taken its toll on those who used to prepare meals at home. Some have come to rely on so-called fast food. Your future customers appreciate "slow food" when they dine out, but they will also respond enthusiastically to your fast lunch service if your place serves good stuff. The prepared food counters at markets are their other source of better meals during their event-filled daily lives.

Recent changes in our culture that are favorable to your future success include the return of bakeries with real bread, which had largely disappeared in the United States. Worldwide travel and ethnic shifts in the North American population have exposed more Americans to the delights of cuisines from other continents. The availability of overnight or two-day shipping brings delicacies to any city, including live Maine lobsters to Albuquerque.

Even the negative aspects of some changes can work to your advantage. Customers appreciate a highly attentive, well-trained staff. Some larger chain restaurants achieve this, but a franchise operator may fall short of what you can accomplish with your team. Although the widespread acceptance of credit cards has increased consumer debt levels, the speed with which your transactions are now processed has also opened a new way to publicize your place and attract patrons. In chapter 11, I describe one such scheme that uses behind-the-scenes credit card processing to offer "club discounts."

The extraordinary worldwide connection among intelligent and interesting people that is facilitated by the Internet offers you new ways to learn and to find the resources that you need. Some of that potential is discussed in this new edition, but there are as yet unimagined innovations that could make the world even smaller during the next 25 years.

The corporate scandals taking place in these first years of the new century have exposed the worst nature of corporate greed and government leniency toward manipulated financial data. Opening your own restaurant offers you a real opportunity to make what used to be called "an honest living." When you place a well-prepared, attractive meal in front of your customer, there is no amount of spin, hyperbole, or creative accounting that will make it any better. Those of us who would prefer a society that does not tolerate spinmeisters are a growing voice in the population, and we, along with our children and grandchildren, want to eat in your kind of place.

We can see by your products that you and your suppliers have done your best to give honest value. Your servers will reflect and describe that effort. Perhaps you will become known for your use of food grown without pesticides, chemical additives, or genetically modified seeds and hormones. Those who appreciate and want to preserve our bountiful fields and waters will become your loyal customers. I can think of no better reason for creating your restaurant.

So You Think You Should Open a Restaurant?

YOU HAVE ALWAYS WANTED to open a little restaurant. Good ones remain in demand almost everywhere. But those who aspire to cook for and serve the discerning restaurant patron must survive pitfalls as many and varied as the people who open restaurants and the places that need them. The purpose of this opening chapter is, frankly, to discourage you from acting out your fantasy—or someone else's—unless you and your partner have taken the necessary steps to prepare yourselves. If you are not a graduate of a culinary arts program employed full-time in food service, your friends, who delight in your wonderfully warm parties with delicious food and drinks, may be urging you to open your own place. Do not listen to them. If you have any restaurant experience, you probably already realize that many years would pass before you would spend another full evening with them, either as host or guest, if you were to do so.

Are you the sort of person who looks forward to a two- or three-day weekend, when you can forget your workday chores and do something different, exciting, out of town? Forget that. When you run a restaurant, even if you serve an industrial park clientele weekday breakfasts and lunches, you will be either too tired to enjoy an active weekend or you will find unfinished work that takes up much of your weekend time.

Perhaps you have been thinking for several years about how it will be when you get your own place and "run it right." Well, you have persistence, and that is a good sign. You will need more of it than you imagined. Let's review some of the more discouraging aspects of the restaurant business first.

The Importance of Location

Where will you open your restaurant? If you live in a city, one place is as bad as another, or as good. A surprising number of factors are relevant— neighborhood, proximity of other attractions, transportation, parking, zoning, previous occupancy, and ownership or leasehold, to name a few. Once you decide which location you would prefer, be prepared to go through the selection process again. Invariably, your potential landlord will believe he is doing *you* a favor by letting you open a wonderful restaurant in his shopping center, or by letting you remodel his fifty-year-old building on Decrepit Street. Rest assured—he will ask, nay, demand, an unrealistic rent. Should he happen to own a building of previous restaurant occupancy and some of the equipment is still in it, he will offer to let you rent the whole package for a mere pittance—12 percent of your gross monthly sales or $12,000, whichever is greater.

Having a good sense of humor will not guarantee your success in this business, but it doesn't hurt. A prominent restaurateur once told me, "My people are always having either a 'day off' or an 'off day.'" A few years earlier, one of his employees who was having an "off day" shot him. With luck, this won't happen to you. If it does, try to keep your sense of humor.

Unless you are very rich, you cannot simply open your pride and joy just anywhere. Selecting the place to change your life is a matter for serious consideration. Your final decision on undertaking the whole crazy idea must hinge on whether you can get the location and type of building you want.

Changing Your Lifestyle

Your decision to go ahead with this restaurant project augurs a change in your way of life that you may actually anticipate with pleasure. Perhaps you will move out of the city back to your hometown, where the schools are less crowded, or to a resort community in a lovely spot. But are you ready to make the change from having a steady, familiar job with regular paychecks, a credit union, and group health and life insurance to becoming a small business operator who can't even afford workers' compensation in case you accidentally serve your fingertip in a Caesar salad? Are you ready to switch from eating your own or your spouse's cooking, with its nice variety of dishes to suit your respective moods, to a choice of leftovers from the night's servings? There are advantages to being the only good restaurant in the small town in which you have chosen to make your culinary mark. But if yours is the only good eating place in town, you are one of the losers when you want to eat out on your night off. And, believe me, you must have a night off. You will want to eat someone else's cooking on that night, whether or not you are the chef at your place. Possibly you will be rescued by a reasonably good place in an adjacent town, but don't count on it.

You will not know the true meaning of the word "exhaustion" until you have opened your own restaurant.

Do you have school-age children? Unless you serve breakfast and lunch only, you will not see the children much after school; in the evenings when you serve dinner, you will be too busy. You may think you can compensate for the loss of time with your child as other working parents do, but the restaurant business is too all consuming to allow that dream to become a reality if both parents are actively engaged in the business. Ponder this: Without exception, every adult I asked whose parents had a restaurant when they were children said they would never run one themselves! That should tell you something.

Let it be understood at the outset: Your lifestyle will alter in such basic and drastic ways that you may not recognize that you have a life at all. If you are in a community that loves your place more than any other, you may be able to solve that problem, to an extent, by remaining open only four or five days per week. Such hours permit a little life of sorts. Other restaurant owners solve it by closing or selling out after a few years. Some just get sick and die. Some even burn the place down and collect the insurance, if any, or go to jail. (There's a lifestyle change!)

I leave this topic with one more thought. No one but another restaurant person will ever understand why you would prefer not to open seven days per week, serving three meals per day. But in most cities and towns, your competition will be open every day. If your success allows you to set the hours you want, and you are asked by an overwrought motel manager why you close Mondays *and* Tuesdays, you will learn to answer in a steady voice. Keep your hands in your pockets where the questioner cannot see your clenched fists.

There is something about the pleasure of eating a home-cooked meal served in a friendly manner by a happy person that evokes memories of childhood. The best part is that it is a happy experience, even if your childhood wasn't.

Your Personality

Wanting to open a restaurant says something about you right off the bat. You have a strong character, you are creative, and you seek independence. Your own restaurant will offer you a number of opportunities to express your unique talents. The décor and ambiance of your place, the wines, the style of service, and, of course, the menu and taste of the food will all reflect you as a person, your heritage, and your own likes and dislikes. Having recognized this, you need to reflect on a few other aspects of restaurant life.

Have you ever had to put up with a partner for 10 hours or more a day? Do you think you can stand to listen to each other discuss the business during much of your other time together, at least at first? Most restaurant owners (or any business partners), especially those who live together, learn to avoid constant discussion of problems and unfinished business during off hours. But in the beginning, when there is so little free time, it is unavoidable. Are you wise enough to escape the disastrous consequences?

In an interview by Julia Wilkinson published in the *Washington Post Magazine*, Ralph Nader revealed that he worked as a short-order cook in his family's restaurant in Winsted, Connecticut. He credited his father's customers, who were from all walks of life, with his own later concerns for what working people do to live. But he also learned, from his immigrant father's outspoken criticism of what society needed to correct or improve, that there is more to being in business than just money in the cash register. There is also a civic responsibility.

Being a restaurateur doesn't exempt you from ordinary people's family life problems; in many respects, it will exacerbate those that already exist. If you already have good communication skills in your relationship, it will be a little easier to cope. If you don't but think you do, try talking about all the reasons why you want to make the drastic changes you are contemplating. Is it to express your creativity and realize greater independence, or are you just tired of each other?

Let's suppose you have and can keep a strong, loving relationship that will weather the coming storms. How do you get along with the public? Have you ever had to, in your previous business or occupation? You will have little choice about it in your new profession. Either you must run so excellent a restaurant that you can afford to be eccentric and reject all those customers whose behavior you will not tolerate, or you will have to tolerate—all kinds. Drunks who appear sober as they enter and are seated will then begin to abuse the server or the nice people at the next table. Militant cell phone users will annoy other diners who don't want to be disturbed while eating. There are innumerable wise guys who complain vociferously about a tough steak *after* they have eaten all of it. There are noodniks who call you in the midst of a madhouse evening to ask you what your hours are for Sunday brunch and what sort of food you specialize in. There is an entire tribe that travels around and always comes in at 11:15 A.M.—15 minutes after you've stopped serving the breakfast menu. They insist on having poached eggs rather than any of the delicious items on your lunch menu.

Employee relations also require consummate skill. Picture your quiet, perhaps elegant dining room and your demure new waitress who started work yesterday and is still scared to death. A former waitress—a regular Valkyrie—who expected to be rehired when business picked up for the summer, declaims loudly in a fit of pique when Fraidy Cat approaches her table, "This place stinks! They were supposed to hire me back!" A few minutes later, still shaken, you discover that the dishwasher, whom you have repeatedly warned to keep his hands out of the food, is sneaking handfuls of grated cheese.

In other words, are you ready for public and employee relations at their most basic? Think about it. A long time.

Managing the Money

How are you at handling money? The cash flow of a restaurant can be very deceiving to the new businessperson. By simply looking at large receipts from a busy day's effort you may conclude that you have made a good profit, when, in fact, you barely broke even. In seasonal locations it is very easy for you to forget, in the middle of booming business, that right after Labor Day everything comes to a screeching halt. It is terribly easy to become overextended.

For every dollar of employee wages paid, you must set aside at least another 14 cents to cover the employer's portion of Social Security and Medicare, federal and state unemployment insurance, and mandatory workers' compensation coverage. There are also withholding taxes and other not obvious overhead costs. Will you be collecting state sales tax in your state? The quarterly and yearly forms on which you must report all of the above seem endless and often incomprehensible, especially when you start trying to decide from a government publication whether or not to include tips and employee meals when computing the figure called for by some particular form. And the form requires you to differentiate between your regular employees and your own minor children, who are exempt from certain taxes. The bookkeeper will do it, you say? Yes, but who will check on the bookkeeper? And can you afford a certified public accountant when you are first getting started? (Can you afford *not* to have a CPA is a much better question.)

If there are to be two managers for your restaurant, whether spouses or partners, how well do you two agree on money matters? Do you have the same goals for using your money if you make a profit? For example, will one of you wisely intend to reinvest some of your profits to make needed improvements in the place, only to discover after a year of hard work that the other one wants to take a much-needed cruise to the Caribbean? Are you ready for the old ice machine to break down again, or can you spend the $1,200 necessary for a replacement, which will take a little bit longer to break down? Money differences are probably the easiest problems to solve when everything else is going well, but they are also the root of many evils in a restaurant. After all, you are trying to make a lot of money with all that creativity, and you really don't want to share it with anyone who doesn't deserve it, right? Maybe you feel that you work a lot harder than your partner. That sentiment alone is enough to break up a good relationship. Don't start thinking that it is your partner's fault that you didn't get what you expected or that you did what you never intended to do.

If you must borrow money to start your restaurant, you must pay it back on schedule, without fail. If you are not certain of your own ability to repay the loan, try to do without it. And be wary of whom you approach to finance your plans. Invariably, the wealthy person who is ready to lend money or invest in a good enterprise will end up trying to tell you just how to run it. There is more on this subject in the next chapter.

You have plenty of hard thinking to do before you take the plunge. But if you can answer "yes" to all of the following questions, it is probably safe to go ahead with your plans to open a small restaurant.

- Are there important goals for which you are willing to work extremely hard—in addition to the desire for money—that you will fulfill by opening your own restaurant?

- Are you and your family ready for drastic but potentially exciting changes in your lifestyle?

- Are you (and your partner) willing to take a major personal risk while you determine whether or not you have what it takes to make your new career work?

- Do you have any related experience? If not, have you arranged to get the necessary training that will enhance the odds of your having success?

- Do you have a good idea of the type of food you will be best at serving, and does the public in the area where you wish to locate need a restaurant serving that food?

- Do you have enough capital to start a high-risk business and survive the first difficult years?

2

Getting Ready to Do It

S O WHERE DO YOU START, once you have made the decision to change your life? Do not start by buying restaurant equipment. There are a few important steps you should take before you commit yourself to any specific location or hardware. The investment these steps require is well worth your time, your effort, and the cost of formal instruction.

- Get training from whatever sources are most conveniently available to you, such as at a culinary arts institute, at a local college or university, or by working in a restaurant kitchen, if you and your partner have never previously worked in commercial food service jobs.

- Prepare your tentative meal plans and menus. This is a prerequisite for site selection, determining your equipment needs, and discussions with advisers.

- Based on your initial meal plans and analysis of your desired community location, prepare the first draft of a formal business plan. A sample outline with a discussion of the purpose of the plan is offered below.

- Visit equipment dealers and auctions to learn the cost and availability of the types of equipment you need and the likely capital outlay.

Get Training and Restaurant Experience

Are you really qualified to operate your own restaurant? Have you or has anyone in your family ever worked in any aspect of food service? Cafeteria work in college doesn't count. It is a rare school cafeteria where anyone actually cares whether the customer gets his or her money's worth. If you have never cooked, or been a server, or worked in the kitchen or dining room of a commercial eating establishment, you had better get a job doing just that or have formal training before you proceed any further. There is no substitute for experience. To help you find formal training, just do an Internet search with keywords such as "culinary school" to find Web sites that list culinary arts training opportunities for every state in the union plus territories.

Even in a bad restaurant, you will learn a great deal that will be of value to you. You might learn what it means not to keep a clean kitchen. You can learn to appreciate a refrigerator that smells good and to understand the need for vermin control. But the most important lesson is the value of teamwork in all aspects of restaurant operation and the necessity for developing step-saving habits. Restaurant people are physically vulnerable to the effects of long hours and hard work on their legs, feet, and backs. The properly planned kitchen and dining room are designed to minimize the incidence of varicose veins, midnight leg cramps, and chronic lower back pain.

Panic among kitchen personnel is best avoided by teamwork, encouragement, humor, and leadership from the seasoned veterans of past panics. The chef is the key to this process.

If possible, once you have your job, spend time doing many different tasks in the place, even if you have to volunteer. Work as a busperson or dishwasher to start with. Move on to serving or assisting in the kitchen, if you can. In each job, no matter how physically demanding, you will learn the effects of good or poor teamwork. If possible, work for at least a week in each position, and preferably for several weeks. Never hesitate to help the dishwasher if you are a busperson or server. Stay an extra half hour after your shift (or arrive half an hour early) to help in the kitchen, just to pick up the feel of working there. You will undoubtedly reap a double benefit. Your coworkers and employer will appreciate your helpfulness and concern.

How long should you work in someone else's restaurant? That depends on your own family circumstances and your success in finding a good location for your own place. But, in fairness to your employer (if you are working for pay rather than volunteering at a friend's place), you should plan on being there for at least four months. It takes three to six months for an inexperienced employee to be fully broken in at any restaurant.

Your Menu Determines Your Income

It may seem premature to try to set your menu and operating hours at this early stage, but there are good reasons for doing so. What you serve at your restaurant will determine what you can earn and spend; you should make up a tentative menu to establish in your mind how extensive the operation will be. This exercise will assist you in preparing your business plan. The planning process will inform and clarify your answers to questions from equipment people, owners of possible restaurant sites, and small-business advisers. It will also form the basis for your initial discussions with local food suppliers.

Once you have decided on the kinds of meals you will serve, and whether you will serve beer and wine or liquor, you must set an approximate price range for your meals. Then you can make an estimate of the expected gross income, which in turn will determine your building rental or purchase budget.

Your prices should be competitive with those of other restaurants in the general area, even if you plan to serve a different kind of food. Obviously, at this early stage you will have to use rough figures for factors such as the number of tables you will have and the number of meals per day you will serve. Estimate these numbers conservatively, then project your weekly gross intake and your monthly and yearly gross, based on how many weeks per year you plan to operate. One way to get a handle on what numbers are realistic is to observe what is going on at a popular restaurant in your target area. Make notes about table usage and turnover rates per table both on two slow days and on two busy days. Average the numbers to get a value for the number of meals served at each table on a typical day. Then cut the figure in half to account for your likely first year of operation.

For example, let us assume that you will have 25 tables, and that the typical day will result in two and a half meals per table. If the average price of a meal with beverage is $21, and you operate seven days per week but close for two weeks in any year, then:

25 tables x 2.5 meals x $21 = $1,312 daily gross income

$1,312 x 7 days x 50 weeks = $459,000 yearly gross income

If you use the standard rule of thumb that about 8 percent of your gross income can be spent for rent or for loan retirement and property taxes, then you should budget about $37,000 per year for that purpose. In some areas, property costs can require you to use a higher percentage. This subject is treated more extensively in chapter 11.

If you find an especially good location that may increase your chances of serving more meals per table per day, a higher rent budget may be justified. You might assume that a larger amount of usable dining room space would also justify higher rent, but this is not always the case. Remember, you want to open a small restaurant so you can keep tight control. You might decide to make part of the space into a private dining room or banquet facility, then attract business for it. Catering to banquets, however, is not always worth the added headaches; it will not be lucrative unless there is a great demand for such facilities in the area. And when the separate room is not needed for a group, it may be difficult to use it for regular dining.

If you happen to find a particularly good building with more space than you need for your dining room, you can consider creating a related business enterprise in the extra space. A small jewelry or gift shop, an art gallery, or a boutique might do well, for example. A retail outlet for special food items such as baked goods could be established. Or you might set up a separate dessert and ice cream shop to serve those who eat dinner at home but like to go out for dessert. Maybe you could open a wine and cheese or coffee bar. Use your imagination. But remember that most such enterprises will contribute little toward paying the rent.

The cost of labor to cover the operation will swallow up most of the income, at least in the beginning.

A Formal Business Plan

You may be an accomplished cook or a graduate of a culinary arts institute with a diploma and a folder full of references. But those items will not get you the loan or financial backing you must have to open a new restaurant or buy an existing one. Maybe you already have sufficient capital committed to your enterprise and you don't need a loan or a mortgage to buy the property. Nevertheless, you should prepare a well-written, concise business plan that tells your story to a reader who knows little or nothing about your talents. Several reasons for doing so make the effort well worth it. If you can describe the salient facts about your plans, then you probably have thought carefully through the steps and potential pitfalls. If you are stymied by writing a plan, maybe you have more homework to do. Even if you don't write well, you still need to be able to convey your ideas cogently. You may wish to get formal advice from a business consultant who specializes in small restaurants. Ask to see some prior restaurant business plans the consultant has prepared. When did the place open and is it still there?

Another reason for preparing a written business plan is to get a line of credit for your operation, which will enable you to respond to unexpected emergencies or opportunities. Lenders, such as the bank where you will have your business checking account, want your business. You should take steps to obtain a line of credit as a precaution, even if you end up borrowing very little and repaying it quickly. Such a line of credit is separate from any small-business loan or mortgage you may have also arranged.

What constitutes a reasonable format for a small-restaurant business plan? Your plan should clearly state what type of food you will serve and what meals and hours of service you will offer. The document should contain basic information that shows your rationale for the location, the numbers that fit your food plan, and the type of clientele you have targeted. List and discuss other major considerations you are prepared to confront and features that you plan to implement to create a successful enterprise. The plan can be organized in various ways. One outline is given below, but you can adapt your plan to fit any situation. The plan should be written in the first person.

Sample Business Plan Outline

STATEMENT OF PURPOSE AND EXECUTIVE SUMMARY. This section should be limited to one page and describe the type of restaurant you will create. If you are taking over an existing place, summarize the changes you will make and why. Describe who will patronize your business, especially if it is in a seasonal area, and from where you will draw your customers. State what your establishment will offer that is currently lacking. Briefly cover what your projections are for business volume and gross profit margin and predict a time-oriented intent to reinvest profits or improve the business.

Briefly cover your food service qualifications and who will be the on-site manager. Refer the reader to Appendix A.

If you have already secured a business location, describe it in square feet and amenities, as well as its surroundings. Otherwise, state what area of the region you expect to serve. If you have a lease, summarize the terms. For purchase, give the price and other details, such as mortgage financing. If you have appraisal figures or other business analysis in dollar terms, mention them. Refer the reader to Appendix D for details. Note

---

Business Plan Outline

Statement of Purpose and Executive Summary
Location Rationale and Competitive Analysis
Marketing Strategies: Clientele, Products and Services,
     Pricing, and Growth Potential
Ownership and Management
Financial Data and Projections
Appendix A: Principals' Resumés
Appendix B: Representative Menu or Food Items
Appendix C: Equipment and Furnishings List
Appendix D: Sources and Uses of Cash (can be in a separate
     document for controlled distribution)

---

whether you plan to apply for an alcoholic beverage license and whether the location has ever had one or currently has one to be transferred to you.

State that the plan outlines your strategy for the business and your financial requirements. Be explicit about what loans you seek.

LOCATION RATIONALE AND COMPETITIVE ANALYSIS. This section, and the next, compose the meat of your plan. You can think of them as defining the "problem" you face, followed by your brilliant "solution." Your choice of location is based on your prior analysis of where your talents can best be used to meet an existing or emerging demand. (Later in this chapter I discuss prime considerations that must influence your choice.) This section of your plan is where you summarize how and why you made that choice. Your competitive analysis must show that you have done your homework. The competition is either not doing a good job or is not able to meet the demand that exists. If there are only a few other food services in your chosen location, then you must show there is truly a need for your services. Cite such factors as planned growth of inhabitants or visitors, new industries with jobs, or other factors that reasonably point to increased future business.

Help your reader understand the potential for success by stating growth projections in percentage terms over time. Give your sources for the data you cite, such as newspaper or magazine articles, local business advisory groups, and the local people and business owners with whom you have talked. Mention successful competition by name and proximity and state how you will be different or will attract a similar clientele that is closer to your location.

Finally, be realistic about other competition that may still be in the planning stage, if you get wind of any. You should have an answer to show how you will be different or better. By addressing the topic, you demonstrate that you have done thorough planning.

MARKETING STRATEGIES: CLIENTELE, PRODUCTS AND SERVICES, PRICING, AND GROWTH POTENTIAL. This section is bound by what kind of place you are planning and whether it is new or the remake of an existing or former food operation. Tell the reader whom, what, and when you will serve. Be specific about population numbers, traffic, and the towns or neighborhoods from which you can draw customers. If the location is seasonal, define the peak and low seasons and how you will adapt to them. If you plan to remain open all year, state how you will attract local business.

If there was a restaurant at your location that closed or that you are taking over, be specific about what you will do differently and why your menu will have the success that eluded the previous owner. List in detail all the major changes you will make. Be realistic in stating your seating capacity, parking location, and customer turnover when discussing the projected gross sales. If there is potential for additional seating, such as the availability of an adjacent space or outdoor service, indicate what you expect to occur in what time frame. Use your planned menu to estimate what patrons will spend for a typical meal and compare your figures to the competition to ensure the most realistic projected gross sales. For your launch-year projections, take into account that you will have start-up advertising and special offer program costs to attract new customers to your location and menu.

Your specific growth projections should not exceed three years for this plan. You can always revise the plan for future use, but the likely readers of the initial document are interested in the short-term strategies that ensure your survival for the crucial first years. Besides, you probably cannot reasonably predict anything beyond three years. The public taste can change drastically in a short time, depending on what new information comes out or what is currently "hot."

OWNERSHIP AND MANAGEMENT. Here is where you identify yourself and any partners as the principals of the enterprise. You should also state whether there are other backers, guarantors, or silent partners from whom you have drawn funds or critical advice or who are signatories on land or building ownership documents or leases. You should describe the qualifications and prior experience of the principals and refer the reader to the resumé appendix.

If you have formed a limited liability company entity for ownership, name it. If the enterprise will be a partnership or sole proprietorship, state that. Indicate who will be the on-site manager(s) and how many part-time- and full-time-equivalent employees you plan to use. Address how on-site management will be covered if the hours of operation exceed the ability of a principal to be present at all times. This is especially important if an alcoholic beverage license is involved.

Emphasize the managers' experience and the plans for hiring and training personnel, along with staffing projections that are coordinated with your growth projections and labor cost percentages.

FINANCIAL DATA AND PROJECTIONS. This section summarizes the figures contained in Appendix D. If the equipment and furnishing items listed in Appendix C are not already in your possession or covered by your lease or purchase, make appropriate reference as to how much will be spent to acquire those items.

This section should clearly differentiate between the launch-year initial costs and the budget for future expenditures based on the profit projections. This makes explicit what your plan is for reinvesting profits to enhance the business. Your sources for capital, including personal savings, backers' investments, and the loans that you seek, should be stated. The figures should add up to the totals that cover lease or purchase arrangements for the years covered by the plan, plus equipment and administrative costs. The major costs of licenses, fees, and other annual or one-time expenses should be accounted for.

Now that you have a better idea of what goes into the written business plan, you can see that several drafts will be needed as you proceed further with your preparations, learning, and site selection. But prepare that first draft as soon as you can.

Learn About Restaurant Equipment

If you are not already employed or formally trained in food service, eventually you will not be able to put off any longer becoming familiar with the equipment you will need to operate your place. Your menu plans will determine your equipment requirements.

Of these, the most critical items are refrigeration and cooking/baking units; dishwashing, workspace, and storage equipment run close behind. And overshadowing all is the proper placement of the equipment to allow the food to be plated handily on serving dishes, picked up by the server, and delivered to the hungry customer as efficiently as possible.

Other Restaurants' Kitchens

With this in mind, you can learn a lot by viewing kitchens in other restaurants. If you take the time to make prior arrangements, you will be allowed to see the kitchen in a good restaurant at a time convenient for the staff. Do not ask to see it while it is in actual operation and do not ask for "a peek at the kitchen" right after your meal. You want a short but hard look, but be sure to mention that your concern is to see the particular layout, rather than to inspect for cleanliness. The manager of the restaurant will be more disposed to honor your request if you ask after making a reservation for dinner or lunch. And you had better reassure him that the restaurant you are thinking of opening will be in some distant city.

When you get into the kitchen, avoid asking questions to which the answers are obvious from careful observation. Do not hesitate, though, to ask the manager, chef, or server what the special disadvantages of that layout are and what improvements they would make if they could. It is wise to draw a quick sketch from memory after you leave, or perhaps have a companion do it while you are in the kitchen.

Equipment Auctions and Dealers

By first visiting restaurant equipment dealers and auctions, you can become familiar with all kinds of equipment while having a lot of fun with your fantasies. Restaurant equipment auctions take place periodically in most large cities; check the classified section of your newspaper. You can also learn a lot on the Internet without even getting up from your chair. If you enter some key words into a search engine, such as "restaurant equipment auction" or "catering equipment," you will get hundreds or even thousands of leads for auctions and dealers all over the United States.

Before the day of the auction, visit the people who run the show for an inspection of the wares. Unless he is selling off the equipment right from the premises of a closed place, the auctioneer usually operates by maintaining a warehouse where he refurbishes the equipment between auctions. If you get to know him a little, he may show you the goods in the condition in which they arrive. You will learn something from that—mostly how hard it is to find a good cleanup and maintenance person for your restaurant. If the auctioneer is a competent and honest businessman, he will take pains to ascertain the obvious faults or missing parts of the equipment, and although you will bid on it "as is, where is," he should acknowledge shortcomings at the time it goes on the block. A refrigerator should become demonstrably cold if you ask to see it plugged in during the pre-auction inspection period. An icemaker should make ice. And so on.

Remember to find out all the conditions of sale that may determine your maximum bid for an item. These include local taxes that apply; the auctioneer's premium, which is usually 10 percent; and, most important, how long you have after the sale to remove the equipment from the premises. If the auctioneer offers storage space, find out the cost.

Unscrupulous Dealers

At any reliable auction, you will be bidding against local dealers in used equipment. If you frequent the auctions or the dealers' own places, you will learn to recognize them. Sometimes they will identify themselves to you in an insidious way.

A soup pot burner looks small and practical when you first see one. But unless you are planning to serve mostly soup and must make it in 50-gallon batches, don't buy one. The burner sits low where it can easily torch an apron, and it takes up valuable space under the hood that is not really usable for anything but a very large pot.

Suppose you are the unsuccessful bidder on a nice stainless-steel double sink with left and right drainboards, an 18-inch backsplash, and a built-in disposal/grinder. You bid $950 and it was sold to the highest bidder at $1,025. Shortly thereafter, a man appears at your elbow telling you quietly that he has an even better sink at his store, which he will be happy to let you have for the price you bid. Invariably his interruption causes you to lose track of the bidding on the next item, which you really needed because it was just the right size for your place and in excellent condition. It is best to learn to ignore such people. It is unlikely that he will sell you an equivalent item at close to the auction selling price. Worse yet, he will almost always overstate the condition of his goods; if you take the time to go look at them, you will probably be disappointed.

If your friend the unscrupulous dealer is a first-class creep, he will approach you casually when you are the successful bidder on a big item and snidely mention that he has an even better one you could have bought from him for $200 less. The kindest thing you can do is to ignore such dealing. It is unethical for a dealer to take advantage of the auctioneer's advertising and effort as a means of garnering customers on the auction premises. If you feel annoyed enough, you can ask the auctioneer to throw him out.

It is always possible that a dealer or another buyer at the auction really does have an item that you need and that escaped you in the bidding. He will seek you out toward the end of the auction or at a moment when it will not disturb you, and will discreetly arrange for you to see what he has. You will be able to discern from his manner and approach whether it might be worthwhile to pursue the offer.

Evaluate Possible Sites

Now you are ready to do the work necessary to find a location for your own restaurant. Of all the steps you will take to ensure success, this is the most important. It may spell the difference between great satisfaction and just a lot of hard work for not much reward.

- Choose the area in which you believe your type of restaurant will do well.

- Investigate all business-related plans for the area you have chosen and become familiar with local laws and zoning that affect restaurants.

- Look into all aspects of acquiring a specific site for your business, including the possibility of purchasing an existing restaurant, or the lease or purchase of a suitable building.

You must accept the fact that, unless you are already a well-known personality, location is more important than any other single factor in your future success. Is another new restaurant really needed at the place you have tentatively selected? The answer will depend on whom you ask, but one way to find out is to go and stay there for a few days to try out the local eateries. If you have no trouble obtaining several really good meals in more than one place, and if they are reasonably priced, maybe your itch to open your very own place can best be scratched by taking over one of the good restaurants you visited. You will find a discussion of purchasing an existing restaurant in chapter 3.

Where Should You Open?

Selecting a location while you are working full-time can be difficult unless you live in the vicinity or can adjust your working schedule. It can take many months or even years to find the right spot to open your business, but this effort will pay off.

Narrow down your intended clientele to suit your particular forte in cooking, and you will have established a principal determining factor in site selection. For example, you may make fantastic omelets, but are you really interested in breakfast and lunch as a specialty? If so, you can choose from several possible locations where people eat those meals in sufficient numbers for you to make a business of it. A central business district ("CBD" in planners' terms) of any reasonable-size community offers one choice. Or, if a small town is your goal, the likelihood of picking up transient business may be the difference between economic success and failure. Does the town have a lot of traffic passing nearby, or is it in a resort area where you can pick up referrals from motels? Is there a main thoroughfare or highway with access to a potential restaurant site? Do tourists visit the area because of some nearby attraction?

Conduct a demographic analysis of how many people live and work within a 5- to 20-minute driving radius of your desired location. Then make a reasonable assumption about how many of that population can be expected to want one of the meals you plan to serve. Residents who work locally may come for any meal, while nonresident workers are more likely to come for lunch and maybe breakfast. Residents who commute elsewhere are weekend and dinner candidates. Reflect your analysis and findings in the business plan.

Talk to Area Planners

Check with the local planning officials, such as the city or county planning director and the local chamber of commerce. You can learn something of interest. But always verify the reported status of planned growth by consulting other sources of information. If a new industry is expected to locate in the town, the public relations department of the company should be willing to discuss timetables with you for a few minutes, if the plans are firm. Real estate agents and chamber of commerce spokespeople tend to exaggerate schedules. They often play down or fail to mention uncertainties and known delays. But you will be able to discover them if you do your homework well.

Finally, remember that everyone with whom you talk in your chosen area is a potential customer of your restaurant. So look good when you call on them in person, and be as pleasant and cooperative as possible, even if they are not. Their impression of you may be critical to your first year's success.

Zoning and Other Local Regulations

When you visit the planning department, obtain copies of the following regulations and ordinances, as well as other useful facts:

1. Zoning laws that specify the districts in which your planned type of restaurant is permitted.

2. Procedure for obtaining a conditional use permit and/or zoning variance, if one is required.

3. Parking requirements for restaurants.

4. On-site and off-site sign regulations.

5. The names of the planning director and the official planning board members or commissioners.

6. The names of the councilmen, supervisors, aldermen, or selectmen (or however the local politicos are designated) that serve the district in which you are planning to operate.

7. The most recent regional planning document for the locale.

8. The name of the local non-official citizens advisory planning group, if any, and the name and phone number of its chairman or president.

9. The names of any local "concerned citizens council" or other community pressure group that might influence your case, should you have any reason to need their support or neutralize their opposition to your plans. You are most likely to need their help if you are planning a new building or an extensive remodeling of an existing building, especially if you are going to make some wonderful old home or a building in a historic district into a restaurant.

Restaurant Red Tape

If your plan is to reopen a restaurant site that had been an operating establishment in the past, that will not exempt you from all the planning and building department's red tape. The most logical time for new regulations to be imposed on an old location, after all, is when there is a new owner or operator of the old wreck. The most common form of enforcement of these regulations is the withholding of needed permits, licenses, certificates, and the like until you comply with or obtain a waiver of the requirements. Statutes to solve problems in sewage disposal (restaurant grease is a big problem), water conservation (restaurants waste a lot), access for the elderly and the handicapped, visual and noise pollution (signs for "fast food" places are an outrage), and on-street parking congestion near residential neighborhoods (if you are a huge success, it could happen!), and to meet requirements for nonsmoking regulations, Occupational Safety and Health Act (OSHA) standards, and other rules all apply to your little place of business.

Even if you don't have a building site tied down yet, do not be put off by the government clerk to whom you direct your request for the information you need. If he tells you to come back when you can pinpoint the block on which you intend to be, at least ask to see the key pages of the applicable ordinances and read them, making appropriate notes. Be persistent as well as pleasant and patient.

Commercial Building Requirements

Be sure to pay a visit to the building inspection department too, if it is not a part of the planning office. At least get the name of the chief inspector, if you plan on having any work done that will require a building permit. Later, when you decide on a specific site and a final design, pay visits to the key people in a timely manner. It can't hurt, and it might even help, if you are especially charming.

Some of the safety requirements for public buildings such as restaurants are useful and reasonable. But others are not really essential. Do you hate concrete? The county engineer (retired last year from the Army Corps of Engineers) who issues your remodeling permit doesn't hate concrete. He loves concrete curbs, gutters, and sidewalks, and you should see his ordinance. Armed with it, he can shoot down your dreams with a requirement for a 10-foot sidewalk as well as a concrete curb and gutter in front of your little place, at a cost of $105 per linear foot for everything.

Let's say you have a lot in the shape of a trapezoid with 250 feet of frontage on Main Street and only 95 feet on the back alley. The county engineer may "help" you by agreeing that it won't be necessary to install a curb, gutter, and sidewalk along the alley—just along the Main Street frontage ($105 x 250 feet = $26,250). So, before he issues the remodeling permit for your restaurant, he will insist on your making a $26,250 deposit with the county treasurer as a completion bond. He will demand you sign an agreement to install the curb, gutter, and sidewalk in compliance with his engineered plans. Of course, the county will give you six months to do it.

What if you don't get it done in six months? Why, then it will be done for you by county workers, and if the $26,250 doesn't cover it, you'll be billed for the difference. That's why he will urge you to do it right away. Costs are going up all the time.

Poof! There goes your remodeling budget. Did you think that the $26,250 should be spent for a walk-in refrigerator and freezer? You're right. But then again, maybe you were never in the Army Corps of Engineers. The only way out of this kind of problem is to get a waiver of the requirement. Don't be discouraged; just be prepared.

Real Estate Considerations

Lease or Purchase?

Do you have a sensible friend in the real estate field who will help you find the property you want? If not, seek out a broker with a reputation for reliability. Here are some of the questions you will want answered by a real estate agent who shows commercial property. These questions should cover both lease and outright purchase of the site.

For *leasing*, you should find out about:

- Long-term availability and renewal options.

- Condition of the building and whether it meets all current codes—electrical (including availability of 220-volt power), water, gas, and sewage service.

- Fire rating for insurance purposes, and insurance responsibility.

- Maintenance and repair responsibility.

- Services available for garbage and trash removal, snow removal, and landscaping.

- Off-street parking facilities.

- Permitted uses for the zoning category, including any existing variances or conditional uses allowed only by permit.

- Agreements or lease restrictions covering use of the building or adjacent businesses.

- Past restrictions on the licenses of previous tenants.

For a building you are considering *purchasing*, in addition to the above you should know:

- Assessed valuation and taxes on the land and improvements.

- Deed restrictions.

- Existing loans and payoff; whether you can assume the loan, and at what interest rate.

- Other outstanding liens against the property.

- Structural pest condition.

- Existence of any conditional use permits and if they are renewable when the property changes ownership.

- Any equipment, fixtures, and plants, if included with the building.

Formulate the questions in your own words and practice answering questions that the agents will ask. Your answers will establish in the agent's mind your qualifications as a buyer or lessee. Using your draft business plan as a starting point, prepare a written summary of your needs and desires, your budget (how much cash you can beg, borrow, or steal), your timetable, and your expectations. You can always change the list or make compromises, but preparing it will save you time. If your initial business plan is in final form, it can serve to inform your agent of your needs.

Remodeling

As a general rule, it doesn't pay to make a major investment in remodeling a building you do not own. If your budget makes it impossible for you to open in your own building, do not plan on extensive remodeling unless the landlord is willing to share in the cost. (This is unlikely.) If you do spend a bundle on redecorating or remodeling, secure the assurance, by means of a reasonably long-term lease, that your rent will not be raised for the first two or three critical years. If you go ahead with substantial improvements to the building, especially to the outside, its assessed valuation is bound to increase. Shortly thereafter, the landlord's tax bill will go up accordingly. (Every building permit that is issued causes an indicator to be set in the tax assessor's computer, which then tags the parcel for "Inspect and Reassess.") The landlord will repay your efforts to improve his property by raising your rent, using the justification that his taxes have gone up. You must negotiate some equitable consideration for any expenditures you make on his building.

Evaluating Rentals

If you are not able to buy your site, an important part of your ground-work is to evaluate the kinds of leases available in the area. Start by asking the landlord of an existing restaurant what the terms of the lease are, giving the reason you want to know. He may refuse to divulge that information, but what do you have to lose by asking? You can always check with the restaurant owner to verify what he tells you. Another source for such data is a local real estate broker who specializes in commercial property, or even a restaurant broker.

The monthly rent specified in a lease may be tied to the gross income of the business, or to the equipment provided by the lessor, or it may vary by month in seasonal locations. But you need an idea of the general run of rents in the area; you can then compare them based on dining-room square footage, number of tables and seats (including counter seats), and the other factors directly related to the production of income. It is also important to apportion correctly the monthly rent of a site where the restaurant operation is combined with another activity, such as a bakery, a bar, a store, or any business not directly involving food service.

Be cautious when you ask questions, the better to determine how trustworthy your lessor or agent is. Learn to ask probing questions in a friendly manner. Try to ask a key question several times, phrased in different ways, at different points in the conversation to see whether you get consistent answers. Take someone else with you who has knowledge in a related area of any sort. This person should just listen and occasionally ask a question to help clarify what you are told. When you have finished your interview, prepare notes immediately in the car or at a coffee shop to be sure you have a complete record of what was said. A month later when you actually go to negotiate a lease, those notes may be invaluable if the story changes. Your friend who listened to the answers and helped make accurate notes can serve as a witness.

Buying Time with an Option

If you have the capital, do not hesitate to use the "option" method for tying up a possible location for a short time. It is possible to purchase the exclusive right, for a week or a month or more, to buy or lease a piece of property. Such an option could cost you anywhere from $500 to $5,000 or more, but it might buy you the time needed to choose between two properties that are not both available at the same time. However, you must complete all the hard bargaining on the price of the eventual purchase or lease, plus all conditions and terms, *before* you sign an option, so that such terms are made a part of the option agreement. Of course, you must be willing to forfeit the cost of the option in the event you choose not to exercise it. But in certain circumstances it might be worth it just to have the time to decide carefully. And the option cost should always be applicable to the sale price or the first month's rent if you do exercise the option.

Do not use the option method if you are simply undecided about what to do; use it when you have two good choices of property whose status cannot be determined simultaneously. An option on the first one will hold it. Sometimes a simple offer with a substantial deposit and appropriate approval (escape) clauses can serve just as well to tie up the property, but this will not give you an exclusive right to buy it, unless you have offered the asking price and met all of the seller's conditions. Thus, your offer may allow the owner to take 10 days to decide, but it is still his option, not yours, to accept or reject or make a counteroffer. If you need more like 30 days, or perhaps several months, to make a decision, you might buy the time with an option.

If you are locating in a town that has any sort of special heritage or historic significance, consider it a signal advantage. Do the research necessary to learn the local history and anecdotes. You will have ample opportunity to make dining at your place even more memorable for visitors by relating a good story at appropriate moments.

Consider the time of year when you make an option offer. For example, if a property for sale or lease is in a summer resort community and you are aiming for a May opening, it might pay to negotiate a 90-day option to purchase in October or November. The likelihood that the property would be sold during those months is smaller, so you should be able to buy the option for a lower cost. This will still allow the seller to advertise and move the property in the spring, should you fail to reach an agreement.

Finally, the specific terms of your option agreement should be reviewed beforehand by your real estate broker and your lawyer.

Don't Forget About the Food

If all this groundwork leaves you with any spare time, or if you have children whom you want to involve in the process, there is one more task, if you are not a formally trained chef. All these years you must have been mulling over the sorts of meals you would serve in your own restaurant. Well, it is time to stop mulling and time to begin accumulating recipes—for large groups, and for small groups, too. Since most home cookbooks are designed for relatively small numbers of diners, you can do some conversion by multiplying quantities of ingredients and sizes of pots and pans. The conversion method of extrapolating some recipes is a good exercise for a child learning arithmetic and fractions, and it can be a practical means of family participation in the effort to establish the restaurant. But it is also useful to find out how many people can be served from, say, 10 or 20 quarts of a dish. These figures are available in cookbooks written for serving large groups.

Some excellent restaurateurs prepared for their careers by catering for large parties of friends and acquaintances.

Unless you possess total recall, you should begin a file of recipes that you will use, including your own secret ones. You can't begin too soon to collect, test, and revise interesting recipes to suit your taste. An acceptable recipe is one that is good enough to be worth the labor involved in its preparation. There are all sorts of marvelous dishes on which you are not likely to make any money, because few people will pay you for the time necessary to prepare them. Either stay away from these dishes or find shortcuts. Serving time and convenience for the chef and servers are other factors to consider in planning some types of entrees. Too many side dishes make serving a chore on a busy night.

This book is not intended as a recipe book, however, either for cooking or for opening a restaurant. There are no proven recipes for the latter—only experience, good sense, and an inherent feeling for what pleases the public with style.

3

Actually Doing It

Y OU HAVE FOUND THE SPOT where you will establish your restaurant. You have decided what kind of food you will serve. You have become a regular at the restaurant equipment auctions, and you have a good idea of the kind and cost of available equipment. What happens next?

Start with the Health Department

The first person you should see is the local health inspector or sanitarian, who should know all the restaurants in the area, as well as all the regulations for them. Come away from your first visit with a copy of the restaurant act or food service sanitary code for your state, and a copy of the checklist used by the inspector in the final inspection of a restaurant before a health permit to operate is issued. Study these documents well and prepare to comply with them. Upon preliminary inspection of your selected site and building, a reasonable health inspector may tell you which items on the list you must fully comply with before the final inspection, and on which items he or she may give you some leeway time. Be sure you understand the requirements, both as written and as *interpreted* by the local inspector.

If you have chosen a building for your restaurant that is the site of a former eatery, examine the record of past health inspections at that location. You may learn something of value in your negotiations with the landlord or owner. If you have not yet made up your mind about a

31

place, but are close to making a deal, ask the health inspector to look at it and advise you how much you must do to comply with current regulations. This information is essential and it should be free, if you are willing to arrange the visit at the inspector's convenience. Even if you intend to build a new structure or add to an existing one, you and your architect should have advance information on what the inspector will require.

The plans for your building or remodeling will have to be reviewed by the health department. There may be certain special items, however, such as the need for a sewer line grease interceptor (or grease trap), for which the building or sewer department rather than the health department has the responsibility to approve. The health department review will be primarily concerned with the kitchen, storage areas, dishwashing facility, maintenance facility, and public and employee restrooms. This department's interest in the dining room will be generally limited to the server station, salad bar, or beverage bar—that is, any place where food or drink is stored or dispensed outside the kitchen. The use of self-serve equipment such as a salad bar or an all-you-can-eat hot table will have its own special requirements. For example, such equipment may not be installed within a certain distance from the entrance to the building. The advent of airborne viral diseases such as SARS makes such restaurant models less attractive and of greater concern to the health department.

You will design your kitchen to suit your menu, and you should have decided upon your probable menu before you visit the health department. The inspector will want an idea of the meals you intend to serve and an understanding of the extent of your menu for all the mealtimes you plan to be open. Why? He will determine the type and capacity of refrigeration you must have to maintain wholesomeness from day to day. The more ambitious the menu, the more refrigerated storage space you will be expected to have.

Insurance Considerations

Fire Insurance

Insurability is an important part of the protection of your investment. In searching for a site, one important factor to be aware of is the fire rating for the location; this is given on a scale of one to ten, with one being the best rating. Any fire insurance underwriter or competent insurance broker can obtain the rating for a specific location, which is dependent on such factors as the quality of water pressure, the type of fire department serving the area and its training status, and the quality and amount of local fire-fighting equipment.

Your fire insurance premium will depend on a number of things, including, but not limited to, the fire district rating, the rating of your building type, the kind of equipment in the kitchen (deep-fat fryers cost you), the type of fire extinguishing equipment you have, and your experience in the restaurant business. Does this last item surprise you? Ponder this: Of all the restaurants that fail during their first year of operation, a significant percentage have a fire. Some undoubtedly fail because they accidentally burn. But many would not have "accidentally" burned if they had not been failing. Moral: You won't go to jail for burning the steak, but you certainly will get into a lot of hot water if the steak burns after closing time.

Liquor Liability

One of the more expensive forms of insurance coverage in recent years has been that for "liquor liability," especially for hard liquor. This kind of insurance protects you in suits filed by third parties for damages or injuries caused by your imbibing patrons. There have been many reports about the amount of damages sometimes awarded by juries in such cases. The injury does not have to take place in your establishment for you to be held responsible in many jurisdictions; the drinker can leave your place and get into an accident later, and if he is underinsured you may well find yourself in court. Liquor liability insurance is therefore essential.

This point is a good one at which to interject a few comments on the serving of distilled spirits in your restaurant. Fermented spirits—beer, wine, champagne, fortified wines, and sherries—are a wonderful complement to any menu. They aid digestion, relaxation, and general well-being. They can be joyous and elegant libations, in moderation. I heartily recommend wine with any meal, especially in places where the water quality is poor. Some of your good customers, however, might very much enjoy having a cocktail or two before dinner, and you may find that all your competitors have alcoholic beverage licenses, which permit on-premises serving of distilled spirits, i.e., hard liquor, especially in larger restaurants with big overhead costs. You may have to have such a license to compete, thus stocking a small part of your restaurant to serve a wider choice of requests. Although there is an inherent danger of the emphasis shifting away from good food service toward higher liquor consumption, the higher percentage of profit on liquor is too attractive, particularly where a distilled spirits license for on-premises consumption is a large investment. In certain counties in California, for instance, in addition to their investment in the building, restaurateurs have paid hundreds of thousands for a general liquor license to allow on-premises consumption of any alcoholic beverage. Such expenditure demands that the owner offer whatever services will help recoup his investment at an equitable rate.

If you plan to offer especially distinguished, single-vineyard or limited-edition wines, consider obtaining licenses for both on-premises and off-premises consumption. With an off-premises license (sometimes called a package license), your patrons will have the option to take home any partially consumed bottles of wine. Some states restrict transporting such bottles to the trunk of a vehicle. To stimulate diners' interest and promote sales of new selections, you can introduce them by the glass, even if they are priced as full bottles on the wine list.

More discussion of other forms of liability is included in chapter 13.

What Should You Budget for Décor?

Millions of dollars are being spent in "theme" restaurants all over the country to give the illusion of long-lost images of outlaw hideaways, Tuscan trattorias, rural Mexican haciendas, rainforest canopies, ad nauseam. The fantastic sums spent in creating a theme do not influence by one iota the quality of the food that is served. They merely attempt to delude your perception of the quality of the experience. It is the food itself that counts; everything else supplements and complements the main effort. Comfortable chairs, pleasing table settings, crisp linens, and interesting dishware and glassware all contribute something, but these accessories will never disguise stale, tepid, or otherwise unappetizing food, nor compensate for bad service.

Simplicity and a feeling of cleanliness are more important than unique and wonderful things on the walls. I do not pretend to be a decorator. My observations are based on comments from thousands of customers, many of whom have mentioned simplicity and cleanliness as contributing to their dining pleasure. Budget accordingly. Or better yet, arrange with a local art center to hang the best work of local artists on your walls on a rotating schedule. Install the proper lighting to illuminate the work. You and the community will benefit from the ever-changing and interesting display. Make sure that your insurance covers the work.

Put fresh flowers on the table; avoid gaudy table candles, menu "tents" that stand on the table, and the other gimcracks that abound in a thousand coffee shops.

If your service includes dinner and your style demands it, you should budget for use of table linens during dinner service. The color and style of table linens become part of the décor, as do your choices of glassware, serving dishes, and tableware. The initial cost, as well as the replacement cost for worn or broken items, should be considered in your business plan. Your laundry service will also offer to supply your linen needs on a rental basis.

Unless your tables are to be used only with linens, even during lunch, brunch, or breakfast, your tables will also be an important part of the décor. More detail about factors affecting your choice of décor, tabletops, and chairs is provided in chapter 5. As a general rule, however, you should plan to spend your decoration budget mostly for good seating, tables that do not tilt or wobble, and appropriate lighting and floor covering, rather than on decoration (e.g., indoor fountains). If the cost of new furnishings is too much, local suppliers of such items will very likely have good, serviceable used equipment at a more affordable cost. The cost of a good used table and seating for four may exceed $900, while a new set may cost two or three times as much. Your pre-planning should include pricing such items from suppliers in your area, even if you plan to take over an existing eatery. An interior remodel is a good start for new management of an old place.

Planning Dining Room Capacity

How many tables will you have in your dining room? The architect will come up with one number, to comply with safety and fire regulations, and to provide enough chair and aisle space. Even if you find ways of squeezing in more on busy nights, you must maintain safe access for customers and servers, as well as the minimum comfortable social distance for privacy. You must also consider your flexibility in handling the typical mix of parties, ranging from the single diner to groups of ten or more, with the majority being "deuces," "fours," and "sixes." For example, it is impractical in a small restaurant to have only round tables, because you cannot easily push two or three together to serve parties of eight, ten, twelve, or more. This may not be a problem to you; perhaps you prefer not to accommodate such parties, or perhaps you have a separate room for large groups. But why restrict your dining room capacity and flexibility?

The fire marshal in your area will be interested in your kitchen protection against fire and also in other aspects of fire safety for the entire building. He will prescribe the number of fire exits, maximum capacity for the dining room, use of firewalls, and requirements in other areas of his expertise. He will want all doors from the dining room to open out and to have locks that cannot be accidentally locked during business hours.

There are other considerations in establishing an "official capacity." Insurance rates may be tied to this number, as may other things, including the number of required restrooms, the monthly sewer service fee, the commercial water rate per unit, the number of fire exits, and, in a few states, the need for smoking and nonsmoking sections in the room. The typical limit, above which you must comply with stricter requirements, is 50 diners. The number of off-street parking spaces required is also likely to be tied to the number of tables and employees.

Off-Street Parking

Your parking lot can be a headache, but it is a necessary one in most communities. If the lot is to serve you well, it should be adequately lit at night and properly identified for use by your patrons. Do not overlook the possibility of arranging for additional nighttime parking at a nearby bank building or at another business lot otherwise in use only during the daytime. You can require your staff to park outside your lot so as to reserve more space for customers, but remember that parking lots that are secluded and poorly lit are unsafe for waiters and waitresses carrying home their tips late at night and for owners carrying the day's receipts. (If you operate where patrons still use cash, a large safe or a built-in floor or wall safe is a good idea for extra cash and the night's receipts.)

Remodeling a Building

Even if you select a former restaurant site, you may decide to do extensive remodeling. Some of the loveliest restaurants are in buildings previously used for completely different purposes.

Building Contractors

The selection of a contractor to handle your building or remodeling project is not a simple matter of looking in the yellow pages, obtaining bids, and picking the lowest bidder. If possible, you should choose a contractor who has already built at least one restaurant in the area, or perhaps has worked on a small hospital or other facility whose operation must be inspected by the health department. Such a contractor will be more likely to do the job to the satisfaction of the health inspector. If you can afford a managing or supervising architect to monitor the work, the aggravation you will be spared may justify the extra expense. It depends on how much you know, how much time you have to devote to the project, and what you can afford to pay others to do for you.

Power Requirements for a Restaurant

The electrical service for the building is crucial to your plan for equipment. For certain electric motors you must have single-phase 220-volt service. Your dishwashing machine is likely to require 220 volts, and items such as toasters and exhaust fan motors are available in either 110V or 220V versions. The 220V equipment is more economical than 110V to operate, but sometimes more expensive to buy. Make certain that 220V service is available in the building, and plan for convenient power outlets in the kitchen. In general, you can never have too many 110V outlets in a restaurant kitchen.

You may find that your small town does not have three-phase 220V electrical service available in all parts of town. If you did not know that fact before you bought a 40-quart Hobart mixer with all the attachments, at what seemed to be a wonderful bargain price, you bought a big white elephant. Avoid equipment that requires three-phase 220V power until you are certain of its availability at your location.

If you are fortunate enough to find an existing restaurant building to take over, many of the concerns listed above will have already been resolved, but you should be knowledgeable about them anyway. Always try to obtain a complete wiring diagram for the building showing where the conduit is in the walls. (The same is true for water, drain, and gas lines.) The circuit breaker panel should be properly labeled to allow quick isolation of the cause of interruptions in electrical service.

Ventilation

Proper ventilation is imperative for a small restaurant. Patron and staff comfort depends on your ability to regulate the temperature and air quality in the dining room. Grease-laden hot air over the kitchen range and griddle, hot air over the ovens, and steam and vapor over the dishwashing machine and steam table must be exhausted. If you fail to provide a sufficient volume of replacement air to the kitchen, you may discover that unwanted odors from outside or from the basement will be drawn into the kitchen, to the detriment of the chef's olfactory and gustatory senses. Heaven forbid.

We had a worse problem. We established a small restaurant in an old home and our dining room boasted a lovely little fireplace. The first time we tried to burn wood in it at dinner time, the dining room quickly filled up with dense smoke. It seems that the hood fan in the kitchen counteracted the natural draft of the fireplace chimney so that air was being drawn down the chimney instead of up. To permit use of the old fireplace, a special exhaust system had to be designed and installed—with a concomitant increase in the electric bill. Almost any ventilation problem can be solved with money and time—two scarce commodities at any small restaurant.

Windows in the Dining Room

A few other aspects of your potential restaurant building are of more than passing interest. If you have the choice of designing your dining room with or without windows, put them in, unless the view outside is absolutely distasteful. Don't worry that if you have only a few window tables patrons who cannot have one will be unhappy. The customer always has the option to reserve a window table or to wait for one. (Besides, the food is the same at any table.)

Americans are loath to walk out of a restaurant once they have entered. They will not go into the place just to check it out. If you want people to come inside because you think they will like it, post your menu on a window where they can see the interior of the restaurant as well.

If your place is on the ground level, it is nice for potential customers to be able to look inside through a window or to see diners sitting at a table by the window. And there is something special about sitting at a window while eating and watching the world go by. It is a compensation the world allows for people who have to, or choose to, eat alone. A window also affords you a decorating opportunity to make your place look more attractive from the outside or more interesting from the inside. Real flowers, even in a window box, are associated with fine dining in the minds of many people.

Windows in the Kitchen

Windows in the kitchen are another story. They can let in light and air, but they may also admit flies in the summer through holes in the screens. The windows also present a security problem if they open to a secluded spot such as an alley, and this is a factor to contend with when you have valuable equipment or décor. You can have bars put on the rear windows, but it is expensive. However, if the kitchen windows look out to a reasonably pleasant scene and allow observation of the rear of the building, they will be appreciated by the kitchen staff. Unnecessary windows can always be boarded up or solid walls can be opened with small fixed glass openings, if needed, to afford some view.

Plan for Enough Refrigerated Storage

Storage space, or the lack of it, is a major drawback in most restaurant buildings. The presence of a conveniently placed walk-in cooler and freezer makes a tremendous difference in the operation and profitability of a restaurant. Refrigeration units are designated as "reach-in" or "walk-in" to differentiate their size and function. The walk-in provides a larger capacity, primarily for storage of supplies between meals and between deliveries, as well as for replenishment of the working refrigerators during busy times. The reach-in box is intended as a strategically placed unit to hold ingredients and raw foods during actual food preparation. It must be immediately accessible to the chef and his or her assistants. The design of the kitchen is so crucial to successful operation that the entire next chapter is devoted to the subject.

Schedule Delays in Construction

Your projected schedule from the start of construction or remodeling to opening day should include a large margin of slack time to allow for unforeseen delays. Some have already been alluded to, such as the necessity for you to post a performance bond or meet other local regulations before a building permit will be issued. Your contractor may anticipate some delays in his estimate, or he may not be willing to predict a completion date at all, but in your own mind you should avoid wishful thinking and add at least 25 percent to the scheduled construction time. In other words, if you hope to open to the public four months after you secure your location, plan for a likely opening in five or six months. If you cannot afford such a delay, your plans may be too ambitious for your budget.

Buying Your Dream
(or Someone Else's)

If you feel that all the trouble you may have to go through in building or remodeling before you even serve one meal is not worth it, there is another option to consider. You can buy an existing restaurant and take over its operation, reserving changes for the future if that seems more sensible. It is certainly a possibility worth pursuing seriously. Your stomach lining may appreciate it. Buying an operating restaurant offers you the advantage of immediate income, an established reputation and clientele, and the chance to see exactly what you are buying before you invest much money.

The disadvantages are equally compelling, but they vary according to whether you want to buy a successful restaurant or one in which the owner/operator is in some distress. That distress may be unrelated to the condition of the business. The owner may be dissolving a marriage, for instance, or may be seriously ill, or may have suffered the loss of a partner or family member who was essential to the business.

Purchase Price

If you want to buy a successful restaurant, be prepared to pay a high price. The more cash you can put down, the better the deal you can make. If the building is not part of the sale, you can expect to invest less money, but the terms and duration of the lease are very important to the feasibility of the transaction.

The tangible assets of the business include the equipment, fixtures, and furnishings, plus the stock and leasehold. The intangible assets, such as the location and the restaurant's name and reputation, are much more difficult to evaluate. The records of gross income and profits in prior years are one indicator, though there is never any guarantee that these will hold true under new management. This portion of the sale price is therefore sometimes called the "blue sky" part.

If the building is part of the deal, you will analyze that factor just as if you were establishing your place from scratch. Here you have an advantage, for you can easily compare the value of the real property with other commercial property in the area. The real property portion of the deal may also allow you to work out a better split between the cash down payment and the secured debt portion of the sale price.

One of your main considerations in making an offer will be your projected ability to recoup the cash investment in full within a certain number of years. Your risk of not being able to retire the debt incurred in the purchase depends on the income and expense figures that are verifiable, and on your cash reserve for contingencies. You do not want to end up paying all your profits to the former owner for many years. One thing to consider when the debt portion of the sale price is secured by negotiable paper (note, trust deed, or mortgage) is this: If the holder of the paper decides later to sell it to someone at a discount, you should reserve the right to first refusal of the deal. That is, if you sign a note to secure a debt of $100,000, which the holder is later willing to sell at a 25 percent discount, you might find a way to come up with $75,000 in cash from your line of credit and operating cash and thus save $25,000.

Verification of Assets

To verify what you are buying, you must have access to the restaurant's books, bank records, and invoices. You will also want to verify the *net spendable income* for prior years by seeing the pertinent portions of the current owners' income tax returns. (It may pay for you to hire a certified public accountant to assist you in the analysis.) Before you will be allowed such access, you will have to establish yourself as a principal—that is, a serious, financially qualified buyer. The usual way to do this is by depositing a substantial amount of "earnest money"—perhaps $50,000. It must be arranged that your deposit will be refunded if the books are not to your satisfaction.

Your ability to observe and to ask questions will assist you in deciding whether to pursue the deal aggressively. You should plan to observe the business operation for a few days, especially during the peak hours, but also on slack days. You should pose these specific questions to the owner:

- How many meals of each type are served each week, and how do these numbers vary with the season?

- What is the monthly payroll? Does it include the owner's salary or draw?

- What percentage of gross sales is represented by food? By alcoholic beverages? By any other sales?

- What is the breakdown of various business expenses—cost of sales, employee wages and benefits, overhead and other fixed expenses—expressed as a percentage of gross income?

- How much was spent last year on maintenance and repair?

- How much was spent last year on capital improvements and equipment? What was purchased?

- Who are the main suppliers for dairy products, produce, fish, meat, staples, and alcoholic beverages?

You should ask for a complete inventory of the equipment, fixtures, and furniture included in the sale price. You should expect to have the option to purchase the existing stock of food and beverages at or below cost, but this is not likely to be included in the sale price. The only instance in which it actually makes a big difference in the amount of cash necessary to buy the place is when there is an extensive and valuable stock of wine. Remember, any transfer of ownership of alcoholic beverages is subject to the approval of the alcoholic beverage control commission.

Many small restaurant owners do not use certified public accountants. If one has been used, however, the CPA's statements of financial condition and profit and loss in prior years, as well as current year-to-date figures, should be of great value in the initial evaluation of the deal.

Once you have answers to your questions and you have a verified figure for gross sales and projected sales for the current year based on year-to-date figures, you can then use the number of meals served to determine what the average customer spends for a meal at this restaurant. You might also plan to make some changes in the hours of operation that would allow you to increase volume without too much increase in labor costs. Basically, you are interested in whatever slack exists in the current operation's attempt to realize its full potential for income. This slack may be in the form of too-low prices, inefficient use of labor, too large a menu resulting in waste, or operating hours that ignore a significant number of customers. If the restaurant is successful, of course, there is much less chance that significant slack exists.

Reputation and Recipes

When you know who the suppliers are, you should arrange to discuss the restaurant with the salespeople and perhaps also the district manager of the key suppliers. As a potential customer, you are likely to be treated with respect, though they will probably not discuss any problems that they might be held liable for revealing to you. If you can establish your credentials and a good rapport, you may get some valuable negotiating information, especially if the operation is in any serious financial trouble. Another source of information can be local business-people who know the restaurant. Also talk with the bank manager where the restaurant's business account is held. Discretion will limit the information you can obtain, but if the reputation is good you will get positive indications from these sources.

If you do some innovative things with your restaurant that prove successful, expect to see your ideas "borrowed" by others. It's a free country. If they do it as well as you do, the public is better served. If they do not, you still have your reputation intact. If they do it even better, get on the ball and outdo them all again.

One of the tangible assets of a highly successful restaurant with a unique menu may well be the recipes of the chef or owner. Try to get possession of these as part of the purchase agreement, but it is unlikely that you will readily or cheaply obtain them. (It might pay for you to eat a lot of meals at the place before you reveal yourself as a serious buyer, just so you will have a basis for comparing recipes later.)

Noncompetition Agreements

It is also very important to find out whether the chef or owner intends to pursue the same career in the area after you buy the restaurant. To protect yourself and your investment, you must extract a noncompetition agreement from the seller. Even a seriously ill chef can recover in a few months. A retired chef may decide to return to the field part-time at another place in the same town. If you have paid a high price for the exclusive right to a well-known name and reputation, and for the recipes to continue a popular menu, then you have a right to exclude the originator from competing with you in the surrounding area for a period of at least five years. The actual radius for a small restaurant might be as little as ten miles or as much as several hundred, if it is famous and expensive enough. A good business lawyer with experience in the field can assist you in preparing a binding agreement. It will normally proscribe the sellers from owning or operating a competing food service establishment of any sort that caters to the general public. It probably cannot prevent them, however, from working for a salary in a place where they have no management responsibility or ownership interest.

Your Menu

A menu serves two purposes. First, it is a communication direct from the chef to the diner. Besides listing the items offered, it often describes briefly how the dish is prepared and served. Second, the menu serves as the most basic form of advertising. Many dinner patrons will not be aware, for example, that you serve a Sunday brunch or a daily luncheon; your menu should announce the availability of other meal service. Also on the menu should appear your name, your hours of service, your location, the ownership, and the type of food you consider your specialty. A surprisingly large number of patrons will request a souvenir menu or one to show their friends. Many are happy to purchase one at a nominal charge.

Menu design and layout are really a matter of common sense, legibility, and simple arithmetic. Few small restaurants have need for large or elaborate menus. I favor separate menus for each mealtime served; but at dinner, I strongly favor using a limited menu with the main offerings listed on a whiteboard or on a separate sheet that can be prepared daily. If you use a standard printed menu, you can still list daily "specials" on a whiteboard or have the server mention them at the table. The menu that varies daily offers tremendous flexibility for taking advantage of special food bargains and avoids the spoilage problems inherent in

Our Place

Dinner

Served from 5:00 to 10:00 P.M. daily
Reservations accepted. Call 666-555-4444.
See www.ourplace.com for more interesting information about us.

Appetizers

Our Own Bruschetta—*Olive oil–drizzled sourdough*
  topped with tomato, fresh basil, and pine nuts................ $4.50
Steamed Mussels (6)—*In garlic-lemon sauce*................ $4.95
Grilled Calamari—*With white wine sauce* $5.50
Creamy Crab and Artichoke Supreme—
  With pita triangles $6.50

Soups

Prepared daily in our kitchen

Gazpacho—*Seasonal*.. $3.50
Curried Cauliflower—*House specialty*..................... $4.00
French Onion—*With imported Swiss cheese* $5.00
Lobster Bisque $6.00

Salads

House Salad—*With your choice of dressing*.................. $5.00
Baby Spinach—*With warm honey-bacon dressing* $6.50
Mixed Greens—*With toasted almonds and cranberries*
  and our raspberry vinaigrette dressing...................... $6.50

Entrées

Entrées are served with seasonal fresh vegetables.
Seasonal seafoods are featured on the daily specials menu
presented by your server.

Vegetable Sauté
  A medley of seasonal vegetables, served over a bed of
  toasted pecan couscous $12.95

Chicken Marsala
  Tender chicken breast sautéed with mushrooms in a
  wine sauce, served with linguini fini $14.95

Seafood Kebab
  Grilled jumbo shrimp and sea scallops with curried
  coconut sauce and mango salsa, served over rice $18.95

Loin Lamb Chops
  Thick, juicy New Zealand lamb with apricot-cherry
  compote and pan-roasted potatoes $19.95

Baseball Steak
  Bacon-wrapped filet mignon, grilled to order,
  with garlic mashed potatoes $21.95

Desserts

Apricot Buttermilk Freeze—*House specialty* $3.95
Cranberry Walnut Tart $4.50
Lemon Ricotta Cheesecake $4.50
Chocolate Mousse $4.50

Beverages

Selection of teas—*Per pot* $1.50
Espresso—*Our own rich roast* $2.50
French Press Coffee—*A pot for two* $2.95
Café Latte—*From organic coffee beans* $3.50

maintaining a larger fixed bill of fare. More is said about the use of whiteboard menus later in this chapter.

The most prominent message at the top of your menu should be the name of the mealtime—breakfast, lunch, dinner, or whatever. The days and hours of service are an important corollary. Depending on how extensive your bill of fare is, you may wish to group the offerings into salads, sandwiches, appetizers, special items, hot meals, side dishes, desserts, and beverages. Any supplemental information about items on the menu should be placed so it does not interfere with a quick scan of all the offerings.

Dinner patrons, because they have more time to order and eat, tend to want more description of how each dish is prepared and served. The main items on a printed dinner menu should be followed by simple, appetizing descriptions of the cut of meat, fish, or fowl offered and the accompanying sauce or stuffing, if any. Do use well-known names for popular entrées, even if you make them in your own special style; fancy new names just confuse the customer. Be accurate in your choice of descriptive terms, listing specific ingredients where appropriate, and be certain to mention whether any dishes are highly seasoned or spiced. But don't go into paroxysms of detail or praise. Often the menu description sounds better than the food actually tastes when it arrives. Your menu should pass this test: Is the information useful to the customer?

Make price comparison easy by listing the price of each item in a prominent position. I favor listing items in ascending order of price, with the least expensive first. But it is not necessary to have a strict order, just a trend from lower to higher prices.

The chef and servers will always develop a shorthand code for handling orders. Some coffee shops assign a number to each menu item, but this makes deletions from and additions to the menu difficult.

It is best not to clutter up your menu with a lot of little low-priced side orders. People will ask for them whether they are listed on the menu or not. If you find that a few are always requested, add them to the next revision of the menu to save the servers time.

Menu Graphics

Unless you are artistically talented and can do it yourself, hire a graphic artist to prepare a basic border and cover design for your menu to provide an attractive setting for the text. You will want to explore with the designer your choices for paper, colors, printing, and the like. Most of today's artwork is electronically created or at least scanned for electronic reproduction using a color printer. Once the design is created, it is thus available for easy revision when your menu changes. It is wise to have at least one electronic backup copy of the original artwork, in case you no longer have the services of your original designer.

A daily menu offers several advantages, if the fare is consistently good. It adds spontaneity to the dining experience and allows people to develop confidence in the chef, rather than in the menu.

Whether typewritten, typeset, or hand lettered, your menu lettering should be of medium size (approximately 12- to 16-point type) for maximum legibility. The main items should be in larger or bolder type or lettering and prices should be placed so they are easy to read and to compare. Before printing your menu, review the final master very carefully to eliminate errors in prices and descriptions of dishes. And check the spelling, especially of foreign words; do not rely on your computer's spell-check function, unless ewe don't mind the possibility of embarrassing mistakes.

Whiteboard Menus

I use the term "whiteboard" to mean any easily altered form of menu that announces to entering patrons and to each table the fare for that mealtime. It may take the form of an actual marker board on the wall or an easel, or a sheet that can be readily inserted into the menu. The key to successful use of a daily menu is its legibility, its availability to the diners at the time they need to refer to it, and the ease with which the management can alter or delete items as they run out. For example, an appropriate board menu may be used to display the luncheon specials or evening dinner offerings on a large board set on an easel or on the wall in your entryway or waiting room. Descriptive details about each entrée may be included. Later, at the table, a smaller version can be offered, listing just names of entrées, desserts, and prices. This allows extra time for people to decide in advance what they will order. If an entrée or other item runs out partway through the mealtime, it can be easily lined out or a substitute inscribed on the several menus. Even if you are not adept with a PC desktop publishing application, your color printer in the office can easily be set up to produce a number of daily specials menu addendums. Using your PC to quickly type up or modify the file to be printed is more efficient than handwritten work, and you will learn how to do it easily when your graphic designer sets it up for you.

A whiteboard menu affixed to the wall will usually not offer a good view from every table in the dining room and is therefore not recommended as the only source for the list. Even one with good placement and legibility will not help the patrons who have forgotten their glasses. In this day and age, you should take advantage of the computer and color printer to make a tasteful daily menu that can be read at the table.

Naming Your Restaurant

What restaurant name will you choose to make famous by your efforts? If there are more than two people involved in choosing the name, it may take months to arrive at a consensus. If your place becomes known for its excellent food and service, it will not matter what you have called it. And no matter how distinguished the name you choose, it will be forgotten if there is no distinctive quality in the food and its presentation.

The name of your restaurant should be consistent with the atmosphere you wish to establish in the dining room. A name that incorporates your family name or first name may give you recognition and ego gratification, but it may also make the business harder to sell someday. You won't last forever, you know, and you may need to sell out. Long names will be shortened by your customers in word-of-mouth recommendations, and also by local businesspeople who may refer their customers to you. Therefore, make sure that none of the likely short-form names can be twisted into something uncomplimentary, ridiculous, or easily confused with any other business in the vicinity. In small towns, restaurant names of one, two, or three words are preferable, with not too many polysyllabic ones. But in the city you can get away with almost anything that will differentiate you from the crowd.

Give much consideration to the graphic representation of your name for signs and printed material. Again, it is worth hiring a graphic artist to design a tasteful logo for your menu that can be repeated on your business cards, Web site, and advertising. There is a special consideration for the name you select if you also intend to create a Web site. This is discussed in detail in chapter 12.

Kitchen Design

T HERE ARE professional restaurant designers who charge a lot of money to design a kitchen, but you should be able to do a good job on your own, with some advice. No kitchen will be perfect, but any kitchen that is reasonably well planned will serve, once the staff gets used to its limitations and idiosyncrasies.

The final layout of your kitchen will be determined by the configuration of your building and by the type of food you wish to serve. If you are planning to work in a limited space that offers little flexibility, you may benefit from consulting an architect who has had experience in designing or remodeling other restaurants. (It helps if that person has worked in a restaurant, too!)

Your first goal is to design a kitchen in which the cooking, meal assembly, and dishwashing areas are each functionally self-sufficient. Most kitchens require one area in which hot foods are prepared and assembled and one or more areas in which cold foods and beverages are handled. The layout of work space and equipment within each functional area should allow the chef, kitchen helpers, and dishwasher to work without getting in each other's way, but still coordinate their efforts efficiently. This means that the most repetitive movements of the workers should traverse the shortest distances between key equipment and people. Movement of the staff into and around the kitchen must follow safe traffic patterns. The layout should help—or at least not hinder—the kitchen and dining room workers in carrying out their basic tasks.

Design Goals

A. Functional self-sufficiency for each area

B. Safety in the kitchen traffic pattern

C. Optimal interaction between key staff roles

    1. Chef to server

    2. Chef to dishwasher

    3. Chef to assistants

    4. Server to dishwasher

    5. Server to busperson

D. Efficient food preparation with shortest path for most common routines

E. Ease of cleaning and maintenance

F. Convenient unloading and delivery reception area

G. Proper ventilation and lighting

Although functional efficiency and smooth interaction of the staff are the predominant goals to be met, the kitchen design must not sacrifice ease of cleaning and maintenance, adequate ventilation and lighting, and convenience for delivery, unloading, and storage of foodstuffs and linens to any of the other goals.

The Kitchen Floor Plan

Insofar as possible, the food prepared in each section of the kitchen should be produced from the resources available right in that area. Also, it is necessary for some areas of the kitchen to serve more than one function, particularly in a small restaurant. The functional areas listed below need to be accounted for in your kitchen and adjacent storage areas.

Equipment Placement

Once you have decided on the type of kitchen equipment you will require and you are familiar with the measurements of the equipment available, the actual placement of the various pieces deserves a great deal of thought. If you are having a building designed for you, or are doing it yourself, it pays to visualize your kitchen space in several alternative layouts.

One way to do this without having an actual building is to make a number of cutouts (or templates) in the shapes of the different items of equipment you will have. These may then be arranged on a large sheet of graph paper on which you have outlined, on the same scale as your cutouts, the walls and doors of your (intended) kitchen. This is especially useful in the case where you have an existing building that you don't want to remodel. The disadvantage of this method for final layout is that the wall space above the equipment is not easy to visualize. You will have to plan your wall space using a front view cutout.

Even after you have arrived at a plan that you think will work well, you may find out that some equipment must be switched around once it is all in place in the kitchen. To facilitate this game, be sure to take very accurate measurements of any equipment you look at in a dealer's showroom or in a catalog. Remember, all kitchen equipment must allow

Functional Areas

Pre-meal preparation

Side-dish assembly

Dessert preparation and
service

Ice making and storage

Walk-in cold and frozen
storage

Dishwashing and pot
washing

Maintenance supply and
equipment storage

Delivery reception and
unloading

Baking facility

Meal assembly in response
to orders

Specialized food preparation
(sandwiches, wok
cooking, pizza, barbecue,
deep-fat frying)

Dry storage

Clean and dirty linen storage

Office space with couch and
safe

Employee personal item area

for cleaning underneath; usually at least six inches of clearance is required by the health code.

Several kitchen equipment and design considerations deserve special comment and caution. The exhaust hood, for example, is one of the most expensive items in a kitchen, though it has no actual cooking function. This is the hood over the cooking area, fitted with grease filters, exhaust fan, and, in many localities, automatic fire extinguishing equipment. If you are on a limited budget, do not attempt to install a stainless-steel hood; a simple galvanized metal one will do fine. But the size of the hood, its clearance above the floor level, and the design of the exhaust system and grease filters are all very important. The hood must extend on three sides beyond the end of the array of equipment under it, and it must have a firewall behind it.

Are you planning to serve deep-fried food? Deep-fat fryers, especially gas-fired ones, are the most dangerous, the dirtiest, and the least necessary items in a fine restaurant kitchen. If you plan on having them, I urge you to reconsider your menu. The special problems of grease accumulation on *everything,* the breakdown and rancidity of the fat, and the fire and burn hazards to kitchen employees make the whole subject distasteful to discuss. If you decide that you must have this item, visit the local restaurant that makes the best fish and chips and the like, and discuss with the staff the operation and maintenance of deep-fat fryers and fat filtration.

A reach-in refrigerator with a glass door and a light inside makes a wonderful night-light for the kitchen.

Are you planning to use an open-flame barbecue or grill, or a wall-mounted grill known as a "salamander"? Some locales now require such cooking equipment to have special air-pollution control devices installed in the exhaust system. You will need to check the requirements with the building department.

Your kitchen design usually begins from a floor plan. A good place to start is with the plan for the floor surface itself. Ceramic tile is the low-maintenance standby for commercial kitchen floors. You can pass inspection with a composite tile in most places, but this tends to require more maintenance. If you use a cement slab floor, your chef and kitchen assistants will probably get varicose veins unless you top the area where they work with portable grids made from slats of hardwood or rubberized material. There are all sorts of products that can reduce wear and tear on your staff's feet and legs. (See chapter 9, Cleanup and Maintenance, for more information on this subject.)

In many places, the health inspector is authorized to carry a sidearm. More than one chef has cooked up a felonious assault in his kitchen, especially when the inspector showed up with an order to close it.

If you do not have a cement floor and are fortunate enough to have a basement under your kitchen, you can install a single floor sink below the floor level. Such a sink is required by health codes in most states to provide for a two-inch air gap under each refrigerator condensation line (which carries away the water that condenses inside) and under the drain from the dishwasher. This air gap prevents contaminated water from entering a refrigerator or dishwasher in the unlikely event that the sewer line backs up. You will save a lot of money if you can install one floor sink beneath the entire kitchen rather than separate ones under each piece of equipment. Some jurisdictions will permit you to use an electric warmer device to evaporate the refrigeration condensation instead. This works quite well, especially for self-defrosting freezers.

The Grease Interceptor

The location of your grease trap is very important for cleaning access. If your restaurant is in a place where it gets very cold in the winter, you should have the trap in a spot where it can be indoors or inside shelter of some sort. The main advantage of outdoor access is that the odor dissipates quickly and the cleaning can be done at any time. The main advantage of indoor access, aside from wintertime convenience, is that the trap can more easily be placed in the waste pipe system at a point where it will do the most good, without being on the main drain to the street sewer. If it is on the main drain line, it will have to be larger and all the waste water will go through it—not good. The grease interceptor should be on a line that drains the pot sinks and other similar waste water from the kitchen. With such placement of the trap, you can then instruct the kitchen staff to clean the greasiest equipment in that sink, whenever possible.

Local regulations may prescribe different or stricter requirements. It is possible that you will be forced to install a larger capacity trap than you really need, and the cast-iron monsters come at an incredibly high cost. Even a trap with a small capacity (expressed in pounds of grease or flow in gallons per minute) will suffice, if you are diligent in emptying it. The bigger the trap, the worse is the job of cleaning it. And even a large trap will not do the job if you do not clean it often enough. You may be able to convince the sewer inspector that you will do the job right and that he should allow you to install a smaller, less expensive grease trap. (The best method for cleaning a small grease trap is discussed in chapter 9.)

Analyzing Staff Interaction

Once you have made a tentative layout of all your necessary equipment, you should examine carefully the limitations that are placed on the chef and on others who will work in the restaurant. Begin by considering the most important element—the interaction between the chef and servers.

Chef to Server

The order tickets prepared by the server are placed on a device that allows the chef to scan all the current orders to see what is coming up next. This "buffer" mechanism allows the chef to perfect his timing and results in all the dinners for a single table being served at the same time, even if one of the steaks was ordered well done. Sometimes this device is a horizontal wheel with little spring-loaded clips to hold the tickets. Or it can be just a long row of such clips on a piece of metal, mounted where the server can readily hang up the ticket and the chef can easily see what is written. In some places, the server simply puts the order ticket where the chef or an assistant can get it and it is then placed where the chef can glance at it as often as necessary. The key here is how easy it is for the chef to read the order.

A second factor is the server's ability to check the order ticket quickly at the time the plates are picked up. The server must verify that the order is correctly filled and must also remember which plate goes to which person at the table. If plates are being put onto a tray or carried on the arm, the order of removal is important, especially if the dining room is crowded and access to the far side of the table is difficult.

A crucial factor in this interaction is the chef's ability to be heard when he calls the server's name to pick up an order. There are also innumerable signal devices that the chef can use, both audible and visual. Ideally, the server should be made aware that the order is ready without the chef having to shout. The layout of the restaurant should allow the server to proceed to the pickup point, take the order ticket, pick up the meal plates, and deliver them, all in less than a minute. In 60 seconds, a hot meal loses little flavor or heat. In 180 seconds, it can lose its "piping hot" quality and the diner partially loses its initial delicious aroma as well. The main advantage of a small dining establishment is that it can fulfill this implied promise to its customers: Hot food will be served hot and cold food will be served cold. Your servers must understand this principle. If you wish to infuriate a chef, design your kitchen so that orders cannot be picked up within 45 seconds after the call.

Food Assembly by Servers

Look carefully at the layout of the work area where food is assembled by the server rather than by the chef. This includes ladling soup, grabbing salad and topping it with dressing, preparing drinks, and setting out side dishes such as bread. If you bake your own rolls or brown prebaked ones, they must be easily accessible to this work area. Many desserts must be assembled by scooping frozen ingredients, adding whipped topping, or serving a single portion from a larger pan, and these can all be done here.

This work area can serve other functions when it is not in use during a mealtime. Specialized serving utensils can be brought to the area as needed, if they cannot be stored right there. The specific limitations of your kitchen will determine how much of this type of preparation and assembly can be done by a server instead of a chef's assistant.

The "Pass Through"

One style of restaurant design makes use of an opening in the wall through which the chef passes food to the servers for delivery to the tables or counter. This design usually allows the servers' preparation and storage area to be right in the dining room, often in conjunction with a counter service operation.

The pass-through design often results in some of the more frustrating moments in the life of the hungry traveler: He can see what looks like his meal sitting in the pass through under the infrared heat lamps getting dry, while his waitress is busy elsewhere. When the plate is finally picked up and delivered to someone else, he views his false anticipation with mixed feelings. His relief at not being served an "old" meal is tempered by the sure knowledge that if she was gone for that long once, she will soon decide to disappear again or to take an order from the party of 12 that was just seated. And she will do so just 10 seconds before the cook places his plate under the heat lamp.

The pass through does permit the chef a measure of control in keeping the plates where they are until properly garnished and ready for pickup. But it forces the chef to handle each plate one extra time just to place it on the pass-through shelf. It is also likely that the chef will pull the ticket—remove the order from the board—and place it next to the plates, where the server can check the destination table number and verify that the order is correctly filled.

Although the pass through is often right up front, one can be designed for a small restaurant without having it visible from the dining room. A partition to block that view can also serve to hide the server station, where water, silverware, napkins, and perhaps coffee and tea service originate.

Swinging Doors

The pass-through type of chef-server interface eliminates constant use of one of the more dangerous features of many restaurant designs— the swinging door. Most commercial kitchen health codes require that the kitchen be separated from the area where the general public traffic is. The swinging door is the answer to that requirement, because it effectively blocks the escape of kitchen noise, smell, and visibility to and from the dining room. But it also requires the server to juggle the plates, or the serving tray or cart, in negotiating that tricky obstacle. The best to be said about such doors is that it is better to have two doors separated by a post so that one can be strictly for going in and the other strictly for going out. This traffic pattern is designed to avoid the inevitable collision that will occur if a single door is the only access. Swinging doors are now required to have a window at eye level containing safety (wire-mesh) glass for occupational safety reasons. But often the server or busperson with hands full will use a shoulder or backside to push open the door and will not look through the window.

The Chef's Domain

The chef's domain is a tight concentration of cooking equipment, work space, refrigerated storage, heated storage (steam or dry table), and dish storage. Today's array of cooking equipment is likely to be centered on a large grill and cooktop burners. Microwave ovens are necessary. (The warming of desserts and bread may call for other oven units accessible to the servers.)

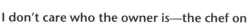

I don't care who the owner is—the chef on duty is the boss in the kitchen.

If you begin with a basic commercial oven, range, and griddle or grill combination, you will find that a typical configuration houses two side-by-side ovens below and a combination of a griddle or grill (available in widths that are multiples of 12 inches) and burners (in tandem units of two, front and back). For example, if you have space for a six-foot-wide range, you may have the top portion divided into six burners, with a 36-inch griddle or grill to the right or left. Or you could have a 48-inch griddle coupled with four burners. When taking the exact measurements for installation, be sure to allow sufficient access on the griddle side of the range to permit removal of the griddle grease waste trough and proper cleaning of the excess drippings.

It is not absolutely necessary to use a combination range. If you wish to set up the roasting ovens separately, the other cooking surfaces can be placed on storage stands or metal tables.

Plate Storage

The "oven below" configuration makes it possible to keep dinner plates warm during the serving hours. But it increases the labor of the chef or assistant to have to open the oven door and pull out the plates while bending down. Overhead storage of the plates, on the other hand, may interfere with the exhaust of the grease-laden cooking fumes, and the shelf under the hood will accumulate enormous amounts of grease, creating an extra cleaning problem.

The best place for storage of plates used by the chef is opposite the cooking surfaces in a device that can warm the plates, if necessary, and also present them at waist-high level. These "plate elevators" have spring-loaded plate holders in a well; as each plate is removed from the top of the pile, the rest of the pile is raised up to allow the next plate to be grabbed easily. Plate elevators save a lot of wear on the chef.

It is important for the plate storage area to be handy to the dishwasher, so that replenishment is accomplished with minimal interference with the chef. Pot and pan storage is another consideration, but it is less critical than plate storage, for obvious reasons.

Chef's Sink and Supplies

There should be at least a small sink close to the chef, if possible, along with a work surface for a cutting board and knife rack. Other cooking and serving utensils of many varieties should hang within easy reach and should be easy to pick out from the entire array. If possible, the walk-in refrigerator and freezer should not be too far from the chef's position as well. The size of the chef's working refrigerator—the reach-in one—will determine how often it must be replenished during the mealtime. It should be large enough to allow the meat and fish cuts that are most used to be stored in the trays on which they were placed during initial portion preparation.

The time and energy of the chef will be conserved to the extent that it is possible to store at about waist- to eye-level height the items that he or she must use for each dinner plate. The more times each day the chef must reach overhead or bend to below the knees, the fewer will be his or her active years as a chef.

Steam Table

Most hot-food storage tables can be operated with or without water. A dry table keeps trays hot without too much dehydration, unless you are serving for long hours without using up the food. (If that is the case, you are in big trouble.) The specific configuration of the steam table or dry table can be arranged to fit your menu needs. Typically, it holds deep bains-marie, or tublike containers, for soup and rice. It can also be set up to hold hot pots of sauce or gravy. Shallow trays for such items as lasagna, eggplant parmigiana, or baked chicken can be taken directly from the oven and placed under a stainless-steel cover right in the steam table. The size of this type of unit will depend on the amount of space you have for it. The minimum width that is practical for general use is four feet, but it is nice to have an extra 12 to 24 inches in your steam table just in case you need it.

Baking Ovens

All good restaurants do some baking—of either desserts or other products made with flour. A pastry table with a laminated wood surface (butcher-block style) is the sign of such a work area. Some bakers swear by the convection oven for making pies and, especially, pastries. This is an oven in which the circulation of heated air is directed more evenly throughout by electric fans, even if the heat source is gas-fired. Some people believe this type of oven cuts baking time so much that it constitutes a significant savings in energy. But these considerations may apply more to a bakery than to your small restaurant. In any case, many are the delicious pies that have emerged from the conventional oven.

Specialized Equipment

If your menu and volume of business require special kitchen devices, you will want to position them as close as possible to their functional work area. Such items might include a 12- to 20-quart mixer, an electric slicer, a meat grinder, a can opener (for large cans), a blender, a refrigerated milk dispenser, bread and bun warmers, a warming oven for prime rib or roast meat storage (handy for a small place where the prime rib is an important specialty requiring several roasts each night), special "broasters," steamers for shellfish, pizza ovens, and the like.

If your menu includes sandwiches, you may find it convenient to have a sandwich-maker unit, which consists of a refrigerator below and a cold tray above in which small stainless-steel inserts hold the various ingredients. The unit also has a narrow wooden or plastic cutting surface running along the entire front edge. The contents of the stainless-steel inserts are kept cool during the meal preparation period by the refrigeration coils below. When not in use, the sandwich makings can be placed inside the reach-in underneath. The assembly of trays is protected by a metal shelf and hinged cover, which drops down to preserve the lower temperature between orders. The unit is designed to be a complete preparation center and is available in lengths from 36 inches to more than six feet. It may suit your purposes very well, in combination with a plate storage shelf and bread storage. If you have an extensive sandwich trade, you probably need one at least four feet wide.

The commercial toaster is a vital part of the lunch business and is an absolute necessity for any breakfast menu. There are new types in addition to the traditional pop-up type that handles four slices at a time, but they may be expensive to purchase or renovate. The popularity of bagels has made the wide-slot units available that can toast thick and thin bread or muffins. There should be space for your toaster(s) immediately adjacent to the sandwich assembly unit.

Food Storage

Storage for staple food items is always in short supply. It is most logical to have a delivery entrance, with easy access from the street or alley, near the main storage room or area. If for some reason this storage area is in a basement or loft, the access should include, if at all possible, some sort of ramp or conveyance on which the heavy cartons can be moved directly into the storage space without having to be carried up or down a staircase. For more economical purchasing, it is best to have storage barrels that will hold 50- or 100-pound sacks of staples such as rice, pastry flour, and sugar. In the kitchen itself there should be shelf space for at least one or two spare cans and boxes of items used constantly, even if the principal storage area is elsewhere.

The health code permits some types of storage areas to be used only if no opened items are kept there. Otherwise, the storage area must conform to the same strict floor and wall surface requirements that apply to the food preparation areas. Rodent and vermin control is unquestionably the worst problem in the use of a remote storage facility. If you are contemplating remodeling an old building, remember that the mice already know it better than you do. Make a very thorough inspection of the foundation and crawl spaces under the floors, if any, and of all places where pipes or conduits enter the building. Even the smallest openings must be sealed with quarter-inch wire mesh or caulking.

Ice

There is an endless need for ice in any restaurant. Icemakers for cubes, cubelets, flakes, or chips are available in all sizes, from the one that dispenses a few tablespoons into a soft-drink glass up to the bin with a 2,000-pound capacity. The price for anything worth having may seem high to you, but a reliable machine is essential. The cubelet is most practical, unless you have a frequent need to pack all sorts of dishes in a cold buffet table for a large banquet type of setting; flaked ice is best for that. The location of your ice machine should allow for runoff of the overflow of water used to flush the machine, as well as the normal cycling overflow. From that location, bins of ice can be dispersed to other parts of the restaurant where they are needed. Remember that if you choose to put your machine outside for some reason, it will have to be protected from vandalism during nonbusiness hours.

Dish and Pot Washing

The placement of your dishwashing and pot-washing equipment deserves careful thought. Besides bearing in mind both plumbing and ventilation of the area, you should try to place it where dirty dishes can be returned from the dining room without going through the main part of the kitchen. If you possibly can, route the dirty dish return path so it does not coincide with that taken by the servers carrying full plates to the dining room.

If you will use an automatic dishwashing machine, the space for it must include room to hold several waiting trays of dirty dishes and pots and pans without cluttering up access to the area. It must also allow sufficient space for the dishwasher racks that hold the dirty dishes, glasses, and silverware to be set up for filling, and there must still be adequate space for the plates to be scraped and prerinsed. The secret of good dishwashing is to place the dishes in the racks with as few food particles on them as possible and to presoak any utensil that has dried food residue on it. If the input side of the setup permits proper sorting, soaking, scraping, and stacking of dirty dishes, silverware, cups, and glasses, then the loading of the dish racks can be done so as to permit easy unloading on the output side of the machine. On a busy night when you discover that you are running out of dinner forks and wine glasses, you will appreciate having a well-organized dish room.

Automatic dishwashers for restaurants have two cycles. The wash cycle causes soapy water at 160°F to be forcefully sprayed all over the contents of the machine for about two and a half minutes. After a short pause, clean water at 170 to 180°F, containing a rinsing and drying agent, is sprayed over the dishes. The dish rack should then be removed from the machine and allowed to stand so the dishes may air-dry and cool. The space on the output side must therefore be adequate to allow several racks to stand. Some dishwashing machine setups include angled shelves over the drainboard specifically for the purpose of holding drying and cooling racks. This arrangement lets you sort the contents of outcoming trays and reassemble them in the cooling racks. For example, if you hold partially filled racks of glasses until a full tray can be carried out to the glass storage area, it allows the glasses to cool properly before use; at the same time, it reduces congestion on the input side, because the glasses can be washed with other items in a rack and you don't have to wait for a full rack of dirty glasses to accumulate.

But luxuries such as special shelves are not necessary for a good dishwashing operation. If there is enough drainboard counter space on both sides of the machine, any clever dishwasher will be able to develop a satisfactory routine. Finally, make certain that your plumbing plan for the dishwashing area includes a water hose connection, so you can use a short hose to rinse out the bottom of the machine.

Your early planning activities should include detailed inspections of the dishwashing setups at several busy restaurants. Machines may be leased if you cannot afford the capital outlay to buy one at first. And make certain, if you are building or remodeling to create your restaurant, that the electrician has experience in hooking up electrical service for automatic dishwashers. It is not a simple matter and has important safety considerations, especially if you have a food grinder with an electrically switched water valve.

If you choose to wash dishes manually, you may still benefit from the use of a few plastic dishwasher racks for holding your dishes while they dry and for dipping clean dishes into the disinfectant solution contained in the third tub of the required three-tub sink. You may have to pay a higher wage to get someone to do the work properly. And rubber gloves are a must to protect the dishwasher's hands. In fact, you may wish to discuss the effects of your soap solution and disinfectant rinse with a local dermatologist and your insurance agent before you decide not to spend the money for a machine. You would be surprised at how small some of those automatic dishwashers are. Of course, there are energy-saving aspects to the old manual method.

Pot Washing

Most health codes recognize that the automatic dishwashing machine will not serve for the larger pots used in restaurant cooking. Investigate early the local requirements for having a pot sink. In some jurisdictions, a three-tub sink is required for disinfecting your pots. Even in the absence of such a rule, however, you may be required to have a sink that is large enough for immersing your biggest pots; most codes do require a double sink. It is possible to get a big pot clean in a single sink. The key is good scrubbing materials, a thorough person wielding them, and plenty of hot water, preferably dispensed through a sprayer device.

Linen Storage

The linen storage area in a restaurant must be convenient to both the kitchen and the dining room. The kitchen linen area must have clean towels, cloths, aprons, and griddle wipes, and space for the bin or bags where dirty kitchen and dining room linens can be placed for pickup by your linen service. The linen service will expect you to keep table linen separate from the dirtier kitchen linen. You will need space in the dining room to store unfolded as well as folded napkins and tablecloths. When the tables are cleared, you may save steps for the busperson by having a dirty table linen bin somewhere close to the dining room.

Office and Employee Area

Leave room for an office. Please. You must have a place on the premises to file your invoices, keep your checkbook and extra cash, and talk privately with employees and salespeople. If possible, you should have room in the office for a cot or six-foot couch. The list of items for an office is endless, but it includes at least the following: calculator(s), cookbooks, first-aid supplies, aspirin, telephone and list of frequently called numbers, employee time sheets, schedule sheets, masking tape, and the other innumerable items of office supply. You may want to have a PC there as well as at home. Or make your home computer a notebook or laptop model and reserve space at the restaurant for its use and for a small color printer and computer supplies. Everything cannot be stored under a counter somewhere.

Whether or not the local health code requires it, you must also establish a spot where your employees can put personal garments so they are not in contact with food preparation areas. This employee area must also provide a safe storage place for personal valuables such as purses. This means that a row of hooks near the delivery entrance, where any delivery person can take something from a purse without being observed, is unsatisfactory for handbags, though it may serve all right for coats. A large shelf inside the office near the time sheet is the best place for purse storage. You will also expect your servers to be responsible for having clean aprons or uniforms, if you use them. A small locker or clothes hanger bar where employees can keep their aprons or uniforms separate from someone else's is also helpful.

Working with Less Than Perfection

Your kitchen will hardly be perfect. You will find it difficult to implement all the suggested relationships among functional areas and people, even in a brand new building. But even in the most badly arranged kitchen it is possible to make excellent food. It just comes at a cost you may not be willing to pay for more than a year or two, in terms of added stress, fatigue, accidents, and frustration. If it is possible to make some changes to improve the workflow in an existing kitchen by remodeling before you open, it will be worth doing. If the kitchen design allows smooth operation, it affects every aspect of the restaurant. What could be more basic than that?

What the Public Sees

T HIS BOOK EMPHASIZES the fine, small dinner house, implying comfort with style, moderate to high price structure, and complete dinners, selected perhaps from a relatively limited menu each night. The reasons for this focus are, in part, connected with the lasting demand everywhere for such good restaurants and the potential for earning enough from even a small place to make the enterprise economically and psychologically feasible. Also, this emphasis allows the author certain economies in describing basic principles and practices that apply just as well to other restaurant styles. This chapter focuses on topics in the context of a wider range of restaurant styles, because the dining room of a small establishment is the feature most likely to vary with the type of food and service.

Furnishings for the Dining Room

Tables

The diner in a typical restaurant sits at a table designed to serve four people comfortably; some of the other tables in the place are sized for two and for six or more persons. Various methods can be used to extend the standard-size table to seat more people, but few serve as well as using a table that is already the right size for the party.

The table surface finish must allow the tabletop to be kept free from accumulated food and liquid residues, and the top must be affixed so that the table does not tip over. The top may be a simple unfinished piece of plywood, to be covered at all times by a thin padding and a tablecloth, or it can be an elegant and imaginatively handcrafted surface, fitting the theme of your restaurant. Some overworked examples of the latter are hatch-cover tabletops for oyster bars or fish houses, and transparent resin-coated tops in which theme flora and fauna or other artifacts have been captured. But I have also seen artistically laminated or bolted-together materials used to create durable and interesting tabletops, including several with wrought-iron frames.

To provide ease in seating and in moving around the table, the top should be supported by a pedestal in the center, resting on a heavy base, or with low, widespread supporting feet. If a booth arrangement is used, the table may even be inserted in a flange bolted to the floor, although this limits both its mobility for cleaning and its adjustment for large people. Tables with legs attached at or near the corners are more stable than the pedestal type, but the legs interfere with chairs, especially if two or more tables are pushed together to accommodate a large group.

Older tables that look like or are antiques allow you to use an assortment of designs in the same room and may contribute added interest to your dining area. But before you buy antiques or any other used tables, inspect them carefully for damage that might snag clothing or affect the table's sturdiness or strength. The tabletop finish can always be renewed—even with plastic finish material. Good quality ordinary used tables may be purchased for under $200, but antiques could cost four to eight times as much. You may do best by combining used pedestal bases with new tops, either commercially available or handcrafted.

Seating

Chairs must be comfortable for at least the duration of a typical meal. And the chair size must permit the average customer to fit under your tables. The normal table measures 26 to 28 inches from the floor to the underside of the tabletop. The typical chair seat is 16 to 18 inches above the floor. An 8-inch thigh space is enough.

The chairs you select should have the following features:

- A pleasing style consistent with your table and room décor.

- Adequate comfort for their intended duration of use.

- The strength to stand up to hard use, even by an enormous patron.

- Durability for cleaning and resistance to stains and development of rough edges.

- Overall size that does not restrict your use of limited space in the dining room—for server and patron movement, aisles, and placement of enough tables to justify the overhead costs for the space.

The last condition mentioned is most easily met by the less formal style of chair, constructed from a combination of metal and modern synthetic coverings. Unfortunately, this coffee-shop type of chair does not always fit the style of an interesting small restaurant. Good wooden chairs, perhaps with padded seats of some sort, come in a variety of styles and finishes.

I have heard too many complaints about the chairs in otherwise good, new small restaurants to recommend that you try to skimp on the chair budget. It may pay to purchase new chairs to ensure you are meeting all of the above criteria. Even good used chairs can cost nearly as much as new ones at an auction if they have a pleasing design and are in good to excellent condition. Consider buying more chairs than you need at first, since you may get a better price per chair. If you have a place to store the extras, you may appreciate having them on hand later for a room you add on or to replace unserviceable chairs.

If you are on a tight budget, however, you may find a good buy in chairs that would serve well if completely refurbished. Or you may economize in a less formal style by purchasing sets of chairs that do not all match but provide a set for each table. This works very well with antiques.

If yours is a more informal restaurant, you might take a simple chair design and build your own seating. If you plan to replace them later on, be sure to get candid comments from your customers on how comfortable they find them. Then proceed accordingly.

Booth seating offers the patron more privacy and greater seat cushioning at the expense of formality in service and your flexibility in changing the dining room layout. For less formal restaurants, booths do offer an excellent alternative to finding enough good used chairs or buying expensive new ones. Some semicircular booths hold six to eight persons comfortably. If booths fit your plans, you may wish to have them made to order for size and color. Sometimes, restaurant auctions or dealers will have excellent buys in used booths, with or without matching tables. You will need to match the dimensions of your dining room aisle and wall space with those of the booths for sale. In this regard, remember that you can fill a few feet of space between booths with conveniently placed storage for trays and tableware, or with a server station.

For some styles of restaurant, even the lowly bench may serve the purpose, especially for outdoor use, informal family-style service at long tables, and the like.

Counter Service

Even the best gourmet menu does not preclude serving the meal at a counter. The informality of a counter allows a single diner to eat his meal in the company of others and, if the counter itself does not take up space better used for tables or other essential furniture, it can increase the number of meals served and your customer turnover. If single patrons are willing to sit at a counter, it makes for more efficient use of your tables. A counter may even suggest special uses, such as serving hors d'oeuvres, shellfish, or salads. It may be limited to the service of soups and sandwiches, or beverages and desserts, while tables are reserved for the longer, more complete meals during peak hours. Or it may simply offer the more traditional alcoholic beverage service, with food service at the bar as an option for the customer.

The bar or counter may be of unique design or historical interest, or it may offer the patron a perch from which to observe and converse with the server or chef during the preparation of special food, as at an oyster bar or with the traditional Japanese sushi. If you use the modern swivel stools with small backrests, you need not give up comfort even at a counter.

If you are planning to open at the site of a former restaurant that has a counter, think carefully about what use you might make of it before you decide to tear it out. Moving it to a different position, perhaps even into the waiting area, and installing some interesting feature for your patrons to look at over a glass of wine might just make your place the most unusual one in town. Consider stained glass if you put the counter near a window with good light. Or a large fish tank might serve in a similar fashion; in some cities, such tanks are available on a rental basis, including regular servicing as well as the fishy tenants.

Outdoor Service

I am pleased to note that in the quarter century after this book first appeared, the opportunity to take a meal or to sip a refreshing drink in a relaxed outdoor setting has become much more widely available in this country. If your restaurant overlooks the ocean, a lake, a garden, or a valley, the unobstructed view and feeling of openness can make your place better than those of your competitors, even where the warm weather season is short.

In Europe, even where there is a short summer season, outdoor eating areas are a popular adjunct to restaurants. Until recently, the United States lagged in this development, but perhaps the smoking regulations helped induce outdoor service. If you plan to allow smoking at your patio tables, make sure that your enclosure and heating setup does not drive away nonsmoking patrons who will be affected by smoke.

If you decide to serve outdoors, you must consider the effects of direct sunlight, which can be devastating to most table and chair finishes. The effects of moisture and temperature changes are even more obvious. Laminated wood will come apart and warp unless the wood was very well dried and treated before lamination. Many resin or plastic finishes or glued-on material such as Formica, intended for indoor use, will cloud, crack, peel, disintegrate, or all of the above. Eventually all colors will turn into weathered gray, especially on wooden furniture and the canvas seats and backs of folding chairs. Oxidation of metal will render some surfaces unable to meet the minimum sanitary standards set for food service. New outdoor-rated equipment resists the effects of ultraviolet radiation and lasts accordingly.

But these and other problems of outdoor service, such as the regulations of alcoholic beverage control, health departments, and zoning inspectors, can usually be solved by careful planning and the use of materials that are designed to withstand the effects of weather. Winter storage facilities are a great help. Awnings, commercial sunshades, canopy tents, and windscreens offer protection to both furniture and patrons. And regular painting, resurfacing, and refinishing of tables, seats, and serving surfaces will prolong the life of your outdoor equipment. As the need has become more widespread, features such as gas-fired space heaters and drop-down transparent tent walls have been developed that allow you to use outdoor space in the evening and during less than optimal weather conditions. Thus you may significantly extend your season for dining *al fresco*.

Accommodating Children and Infants

High chairs are an invitation to patrons who otherwise may not frequent your establishment. Your tolerance for the problems that go along with serving infants and toddlers will determine whether you use and retain this type of seat. If you do provide high chairs, be certain you have both a safe place to store them when not in use and sufficient space at some of the tables to set up the chair so that the child can neither grab at a server carrying hot food nor be tripped over. Old wooden high chairs are nice, but they cost a lot of money. The new plastic types may offer the convenience of foldaway storage as well as a more easily cleanable surface finish.

Seating for the somewhat older child who is too big for a high chair but too small for the regular seat presents a potential safety problem. The traditional padded booster device, resembling a small hassock with a little rounded back, is designed for use *only* in a booth. It should not be used on a chair that does not have side arms to prevent its tipping over and allowing the child to fall. If you do not have a youth chair (a higher chair without a tray) that can be moved right up to the table, try the old telephone book trick or something similar to raise the youngster enough to eat comfortably but not precariously.

Other Dining Room Needs

It is impractical to have to carry water from the kitchen to the table. Even if you cannot provide the plumbing to allow your servers to fill a pitcher conveniently right in the dining room, it is essential that you have a place for filled water pitchers and storage for clean water and wine glasses in the dining area. The same holds true for cups and saucers for tea and coffee. It is a great convenience to have an ice receptacle in the dining room, as well as conveniently placed coffeepots and hot water.

The need for clean tableware and linen for setting the tables is never ending. If you use tablecloths, they must be stored nearby, yet not in a place where they may be splashed by liquids or food particles. The same goes for other place setting items, such as place mats and napkins. If you regularly use small dishes such as butter plates for your place settings, these should be stored for easy access when setting up a table. Be sure to provide a place for serving trays when not in use, as well as a spot to hold damp wipe cloths out of sight of the patrons. You may also want a place for special condiments that are not always on the table, such as mustard, ketchup, salsa, hot sauce, syrups, vinegar and oil, relish, or what have you.

Visit the local antique shops on your day off. A beautiful piece will often fit into almost any small restaurant's décor and can serve you well for storage and delight your customers, too. Moreover, the shop owner may be smart enough to give you a "business discount" if your restaurant caters to the antique-buying public.

All these needs may require you to build special shelves and cupboards, or you might take the opportunity to add some interesting or antique piece of furniture that will give a touch of hominess to the room. A sea captain's chart desk might serve to hold some of the items mentioned, as well as menus and wine lists, or perhaps the large old sideboard that grandma almost gave away because it was too big for her apartment will do nicely.

Self-Service Equipment

The popular self-service salad bars—including those with places for soup tureens, hot bread or rolls, butter, and all the dressings and garnishes that go with salads—have become commonplace in the years since first I wrote. Your plans may include the use of such self-service equipment, or something similar for making your own ice-cream sundaes, assembling your own stir-fried meal, or making your own veggie or fruit drink in a blender/juicer.

Your decision to use this equipment will be of great interest to the local health inspector. He or she will be concerned about what provision you make for what is commonly known as a "sneeze guard." It is also called a "breath barrier," and probably other names I haven't yet heard of. This transparent barrier must stand between the patrons' faces and any uncovered food, to block the transfer of germs from the breath to the common pot. It must be wide enough to work for various sizes of people while not obstructing the view of what you are trying to serve. Such barriers have been in use for years in cafeterias where individual portions of food, such as salads and desserts, are available for selection in an unwrapped condition. But they present a particularly awkward problem for serve-yourself bars, which have already been outlawed completely in many places as an insurmountable health hazard.

Dining Room Décor

I have no intention of discussing all the possibilities for interior design for restaurants; I am not an expert on this subject, nor am I likely to be of much help with any specific style. It will be useful, however, to understand a few principles in advance, if your common sense and powers of observation have not already made them evident.

- *Your dining room layout should afford a view of the entire room, if possible, from one or two vantage points near the front entrance.* This will enable the manager or host to oversee and respond to needs not always evident to the servers. Your use of room dividers, half-walls, and structural supporting walls or columns, therefore, should create a feeling of coziness and semi-privacy without actually cutting up the room into cubicles. The careful use of appropriate potted plants rather than partitions to define pathways within the dining area is sometimes a flexible and more natural method. Plants can also screen the view toward the kitchen area or a less attractive serving station or storage area.

- *The lighting in your dining room must not sacrifice safety to mood and should be augmented wherever a hazard such as a step or ramp occurs.* The natural light from windows and skylights is always preferable to excessive reliance on artificial lighting. Using dimmer switches for your incandescent lights can help you change from a daytime to an evening mood. The more we learn about the biological effects of light on mammals, the less I approve of fluorescent lights, even for very informal dining rooms. Also, you should control glaring light from any source by shades or other means that diffuse, deflect, or block it. In short, it is well worth your time to study the lighting design of as many dining rooms as possible before you commit yourself to an electrical wiring and switching plan and invest in fixtures.

- *Heating and cooling devices must not subject one or more tables to an extreme temperature.* This is a rule that should never be violated, yet it is commonly ignored for the sake of squeezing in one more table. How will you feel when you discover too late that you have seated an anonymous but very influential restaurant critic at the one table with an intolerable draft?

Resist the temptation to use items such as old beautiful teapots, bud vases, or antique saltcellars unless you are willing to part with them. They may not be pilfered, but they probably will be chipped, cracked, or even broken by a well-meaning but clumsy dishwasher.

- *Your wall space is better treated as a backsplash and reflector of light and color than as a display in a museum.* This does not mean that you should stick to bare walls. Rather, make use of mirrors to lighten some darker corners; cover the wall surface closest to the tabletops and seats with a suitable finish for constant cleansing;

and limit your theme artifacts or artwork to a tasteful selection of a few items, instead of crowding your entire collection into the room at one time. If you are fortunate enough to own a large and appealing collection of objects of historical or aesthetic interest, your steady customers as well as your staff will appreciate them more if you periodically change the display rather than plastering the walls and ceiling with them.

- *Whatever decorations or display you employ must be kept clean and dust-free.* A dusty or grimy-looking antique does not stimulate the appetite, nor does a musty drapery or curtain. Even a funny picture or sign loses its impact if it turns out to be covered with dust or fly specks when one gets close.

- *If possible, have one or more tables in your room that are somewhat shielded from other tables, where parties with small children can be seated.* This will allow you to move anyone who is annoyed by a fussy child to another table. You could make good use of a portable screen under such circumstances, if you have a nice one. The screen can also be used when a larger party desires some separation from the rest of the room and you do not have a private room for the purpose. (But make sure that any freestanding screen is stable.)

- *Signs should be legible from across the room, even at night.* There is no point in marking directions to the restrooms if your signs result in most patrons having to ask for directions anyway. The local fire regulations will prescribe exit signs.

No Smoking?

Many jurisdictions have already restricted or banned smoking in restaurants. A careful reading of the local smoking regulations and method of enforcement is the place to start. If you have outdoor service, make sure you understand and can explain whether smoking is allowed there, even if it is restricted indoors.

The rules in your locale may require you to reserve a significant portion of your dining room for those who are annoyed by smoking. Even if this is not required, it is a good solution if you have the room. Put up a sign, or ask each party as they arrive if they prefer a no-smoking section. Your best weapon in any case is a quiet, but very effective exhaust system for the dining room. When the smoke clears, however, you want both the smokers and the nonsmokers to realize that you have done your best to allow them both to enjoy their meals.

If you operate in a locale that has made smoking unlawful, you may encounter the difficulty of patrons who light up in the bathroom, to the discomfort of others who enter afterward. Be sure to post a large No Smoking sign there. The smoker may also loiter outside the front door while others in his party finish their dessert. This, too, may dissuade others from entering. If your site has a suitable place, you may wish to designate an outdoor smoking bench or patio far from the front entry for use by your nicotine-addicted patrons.

What else can you do? Do not sell cigarettes or cigars in your restaurant; offer matches only on request, but if smoking is allowed in a designated area cheerfully provide an ashtray to protect your table and carpet when a smoker asks for one or lights up without one. Display a sign that states what the local ordinance requires, such as no smoking in restrooms. *Enforce strictly the universal health standard for food service personnel, which prohibits use of tobacco in any form while working with or near food.*

In our restaurant waiting room we displayed a sign in a somewhat florid calligraphy that said, "Thank You for Not Smoking." Most people took it to mean that smoking was prohibited. Smokers often asked if that was the case and were told, "You are permitted to smoke, but naturally in our small dining room we don't encourage it." To mollify them, I was able to take advantage of the calligraphic resemblance of the "M" to "N" and of the "K" to "R" and tell them that on busy nights many waiting people read the sign as "Thank You for Not Snoring."

The Cashier Station and the Waiting Room

The cashier station is where you will carry out all the tasks related to checking the customers' bills; making change; and preparing and verifying transactions with credit cards, traveler's checks, and personal checks, if you accept them. Here you may wish to provide space, and electrical outlets, for special lighting, a cash register, a calculator, a credit-card reader, controls for your music system, a paging system, an intercom with the kitchen or other key points in the restaurant, a telephone jack, and a special safe or lockable built-in drawer for holding extra cash or deposits separately from the receipts in the cash drawer. When the cashier operation is combined with handling reservations, the space must be larger, and you will need to be able to see and communicate with the dining room. Most small restaurants combine these operations at or near the front entrance or exit.

If the cash drawer is in the area where patrons wait to be seated, a logical use of the host's time when there are no tables available is to have him handle the cashier's job. But you may deliberately separate the cash drawer from the waiting room, for safety, for the convenience of the servers, or because of space limitations. I have found that it is best to limit the handling of the money to as few people as practical. Variations on this practice depend on the style of the restaurant and also on how busy it is. The less formal the meal, the more likely it is that the cash drawer will be manned by whomever has the time at the moment the customer is ready to pay.

The busier your restaurant, the more likely it is that you can afford a full-time cashier or host/cashier. The cashier can also double as bartender; busperson; table setter; takeout clerk; or regular server for a station, such as a counter, that is near the cash drawer. If your waiting room is the site for any tie-in retail sales such as take-home food, jewelry, or souvenirs, it is natural for the cashier to handle that operation.

If you do not use a cash register that produces some sort of printed record of your sales, you should consult your accountant or tax adviser about what methods to use to verify your sales volume, both for income tax and state sales tax purposes.

In most urban areas or places visited by travelers, it is rare to find a restaurant these days that does not accept at least the two most used credit cards. If you plan to operate on a cash or personal check basis, make sure that your customers are clearly informed by a sign as they enter the restaurant that you do not accept credit cards (it wouldn't hurt to note it as well on the menu) and note the location of the nearest ATM. If you take reservations, make certain that this information is also part of the reservation conversation.

Certain tie-in sales in a restaurant may present special cases for segregating those records and receipts from your table service or consumption-on-premises sales. If your cash register does not have the means for entering a code while ringing up the sale, you may choose to employ entirely separate registers. Examples of such sales include cases where state sales or meals tax applies to the food served or consumed on the premises, but not to food, such as bakery or delicatessen items, sold for consumption at home. Your financial adviser or accountant will know what methods for keeping records and receipts are most practical and acceptable to the tax people.

There is something to be said for the system used in Europe: The customer pays the server, who carries her own change and makes it, and the server is then responsible for paying the house every time food or drink is served. It reduces "arithmetic errors" that are otherwise absorbed by the owner.

What about all those people in the waiting room? Some restaurant owners I know would love to have that problem. It is best solved before it occurs, by making sure the size of your waiting area is adequate. You should provide seats for a reasonable number of people—about five to eight seats for a 40-seat restaurant. The benches or chairs should be placed so they do not interfere with patrons who are there to pay the cashier or with servers delivering a check or payment to the cashier. The seats should not impede the normal traffic through the entry area.

Besides capacity, you want the area to make a pleasing first impression on new customers. It can be more than just an all-weather room for a short wait for a table. Set up your entry room so a customer coming in on a busy night will naturally gravitate to the host or cashier and give her name and the number in her party, or ask the inevitable "How long is the wait for a table for two?"

One way to pay for the cost of a larger entry area is to plan for display cases for small but high-priced items you can sell to those who spend time in the room. (A lighted case is very desirable at night.) Almost any interesting handcrafted item or collectible, whether new or antique, is suitable, but hand-crafted jewelry will probably get the most attention from your patrons. Maybe your own hobby fits the bill. Miniature soldiers, scale-model trains, dolls, clocks, handblown glassware, spoon collections, dollhouse furniture, old documents—the list is virtually endless, and it doesn't have to tie in with your restaurant's name, style of food, or service. It just has to be interesting, unique, or scarce, and not cheap or tacky.

What About Restrooms?

You have as much obligation to satisfy your customers' hygienic needs as you do to meet their need for nourishment and physical comfort. To me, this means you must have a clean public toilet and sink. The health regulations already require no less for your employees.

Countless satisfied customers commented on how nice and clean our restrooms were, and how often they judge the attitude of a restaurant by that observation.

Those jurisdictions that require restrooms for both patrons and employees often also require a vestibule between the restroom door and the dining room or kitchen. In some locales, this requirement is being eliminated for the dining room access. (See below for some uses you can make of such vestibules.) Local regulations will influence the number and placement of your restrooms and, in many cases, what their minimum area must be. Some building codes stipulate how the air in the restrooms shall be exhausted, how the fan motor and light switch shall be interconnected, and so on, to the point where you may wish you could avoid installing a bathroom altogether.

How Many?

For a small restaurant, you do not need a large restroom, but you can always use more than one, even if the regulation says you can get away with only one for your seating capacity. So if you have the space, it may be better to remodel a large restroom into two or three smaller ones.

If your restroom capacity is one person at a time, I see no good reason for designating one room for men and the other for women. Passenger-aircraft restrooms serve very well without such restrictions. Try doing something more practical, such as installing a special grab rail for older people and small children, next to a pedestal toilet, which is higher than the conventional toilet. The pedestal toilet is easier for people with arthritis or disabilities to use. And remember to follow the latest regulations for handicapped accessibility. Dispensing with Men and Women signs improves the availability of restrooms when the demand is unbalanced. Besides, I believe that it discourages graffiti, though maybe not.

Regardless of the number of restrooms you provide, it helps to have the floors made of ceramic tile, with a good waterproof grout, so that you can keep them as spotlessly clean as possible. It also helps to have tile walls or to keep the walls painted, so they can survive frequent wash-downs without pitting. And the bathroom décor ought to give a feeling of cleanliness. If you can afford it, install a ceramic tile wainscot behind the fixtures, especially if you have a men's urinal of any sort.

Urinals Are Useless

I do not recommend installing urinals, primarily because some designs are useless for small boys and because they are more of a nuisance to keep clean and sweet smelling than are toilets. Aside from splashing problems, men are less likely to flush a urinal than a regular toilet. If you are concerned about the water consumption for toilets, there are low-flush toilets or replacement valves that can be set for the amount of water you wish to use in the tank. If you seek ways to conserve water, you will do better by replacing leaky faucet washers and instructing your dishwashing crew in conservation measures than by installing urinals. The automatic flush urinal models found in airports and elsewhere do save water. In drought areas and if you serve lots of beer, you may want to consider that. Likewise for delayed shut-off sink fixtures, although I have not seen one with handicap-accessible handles, so you might need two sinks in that case.

Lighting and Ventilation

Lighting in the restroom is just as important as in the kitchen, but it need not be glaringly bright. Let the light be adequate but not unflattering to the patron who checks to see how he or she looks in the mirror. Do provide mirrors, and keep them clean. It is nice to have a source of natural daylight in the restroom if you can; a skylight will serve where no outside wall is available, and now there are even those that bring the outside light around corners using mirrors in the light tube.

A direct source of fresh outside air is also a desirable restroom feature, rather than having to rely on an exhaust fan. The air sucked into the restroom by such a fan usually comes from inside the building, where it has already become stale and laden with odors from cooking and people.

Restroom Locks

Be prepared for little dramas to be acted out in your restrooms. There is no lock or latch that will not confound someone. Most failures will revolve around an unlatched door leading to an embarrassment, but occasionally a small child will inadvertently lock himself in. A simple slide latch or hook is all that is really needed to indicate that the room is in use; stout locks are superfluous. Many jurisdictions, however, do require an automatic door closer.

Making Use of the Restroom Vestibule

Do not ignore your restroom vestibule when you plan your décor and obtain seats for the waiting room. The typical use for this spot, if it is large enough, is as a holding area for patrons waiting to use an occupied bathroom and as a place to install a public telephone. If you do not take credit cards, it can house a small ATM. Some restaurant owners fill the extra space with pictures and notes from happy or famous customers or souvenir T-shirts available for sale, and what have you. My personal favorite use of the wall space, even in a small vestibule, is to display information on the history of the restaurant building, the town, or the area, and to give directions to points of interest or other data of an entertainment value.

On Music

If you have ever spent an evening in a small restaurant where your enjoyment of well-prepared fresh food and stimulating conversation was completely negated by atrocious background music, then you can appreciate the importance of music in a restaurant. With a happy choice of music to enhance their dining interlude, patrons may well compliment the musical accompaniment even more than the chef's best efforts.

The effect of music on your chef, your staff, and yourself is of as much concern as its effect on your patrons in the dining room. After all, unlike the diners, you and your staff must endure the music all day and evening. Therefore, your system should allow you to select variety as well as to provide continuity.

The availability of compact disk (CD) players that enable you to choose a daily variety of music does not involve a large initial capital investment. The players and properly sited small speakers are affordable, and your operating budget must include purchase of new CDs throughout the year.

The level of sound in a dining room is very important. Subtle differences in sound level can create or destroy your intended mood. Ever since the moguls of industry discovered that music affects human behavior, there have been systems designed to produce so-called background music. The music itself is supposed to be innocuous and the sound level set so that you don't actually have to attend to what is being played. In fact, if you want to listen, you must sometimes strain to hear. This kind of music serves the same function as do pleasing colors in the décor, without being as apparent. In a small restaurant, however, both the selection and the loudness of music call for something better than what is provided by the typical background music system.

There are a number of reasons for this. Music in a restaurant serves several important functions:

- Conscious enjoyment of favorite melodies or familiar performances.

- Masking of private conversations from those at adjacent tables.

- Making an empty dining room feel less empty.

- Inducing relaxation and setting a mood consistent with the cuisine.

- Encouraging the staff to survive dull routine by providing enjoyment that does not interfere with their movements and interactions.

These functions require that the listener not have to strain to hear the music, yet not have to shout to be heard. Ordinary background music systems typically use few speakers or ones with low-fidelity response. They tend to achieve a subliminal effect, whereas one of your objectives is to have your patrons remember the music along with the meal and to recommend your restaurant because of that memory.

Choosing the Music

What music do *you* like? That is as good a place to begin as any. If you serve dinner in the continental style, classical music is always appropriate. If you serve country style, bluegrass may be right. New Orleans hot jazz will do nicely for any lunch and some dinner styles. In my experience, there is no meal for which there is not some appropriate performance of one of the classics. The same may be said for other types of music, from simple folk melodies to modern jazz. The key to appropriateness is more in the number and arrangement of the instruments rather than the style of music. In both classical and contemporary music, loud brass and percussion—or any overpowering arrangement of instruments—are to be avoided; choose pieces that feature one, two, or several instruments that blend well together. A Handel recorder sonata or a Mozart quartet for flute and strings would be better than a Beethoven symphony or a Verdi opera. Violin, flute, piano, acoustic guitar, harp, sitar, dulcimer, harpsichord, cello, viola, French horn, oboe, recorder, and even the electronic organ can all be pleasing alone or in combination. The voice is a very appropriate instrument for restaurant music, provided the lyrics are right and the accompaniment meets the above criteria for restraint and peacefulness.

My personal favorite musician whose work makes the listener simply glad to be alive to hear it is Pat Donohue. His acoustic guitar work borders on the unbelievable (he was the 1983 finger-picking National Champion). He is a regular on *A Prairie Home Companion* radio on NPR. His local concerts and CDs offer both solo instrumental and delightful vocal material. In some CDs he is featured with other outstanding musicians, including the late Chet Atkins. This music from a Minnesotan goes with any food in America.

How to Get It

In the main, you are limited to recorded music on CDs or on one of the newer digital media. The disadvantages of FM broadcasts, formerly acceptable, involve radio commercials, which may be inappropriate for your restaurant.

Royalties

The 1998 so-called Fairness in Music Licensing Act established an exemption from payment of royalties for the use of music in eating or drinking establishments of fewer than 3,750 gross square feet. Larger places that provide audio only via six or fewer speakers, of which not more than four are in one room, are also exempt. The United States is the only country to take away the right of the composer or publisher of a musical work to be paid a modest royalty for the use—in this case rebroadcast—of intellectual property. In Canada, a restaurant that plays music from CDs is subject to the collection of royalties by SOCAN. All other business establishments in the United States have not been exempted as restaurants have. For all such use, royalties are collectible by one of the organizations that distribute royalty payments to music copyright owners. They are ASCAP, BMI, and SESAC. The law may change or be challenged in the case of international treaties for the collection of foreign royalties. It would be prudent to be aware of any future obligations, but the next paragraph discusses a situation that makes the question moot.

The piracy of intellectual property and the ability of computer users to download and share music files are currently major threats to the future availability of CDs (and DVDs too). If the predicted outcome ensues, you may have to create your own CDs to play on your equipment by using a broadband access to the Internet music services that will offer the music you want at a reasonable fee. If you do not have the means to "burn" your own CD or the desire to spend time doing so, you should be able to find a computer service that will do it for you for a fair price. The advantage of such a scheme is that you can select exactly the type and mixture of music that you would like to hear at a particular time of day or evening. Your collection of such tailored CDs will require little attention during busy hours.

Live Performers

My most cherished memories include evenings spent in a restaurant listening to musicians playing classical and flamenco guitar, mandolin, violin, flute, piano, and harp. Of these memories, the solo performances by a flamenco or classical guitarist stand out as the epitome of pleasurable accompaniment to a relaxing evening meal—as much as a bottle of the finest wine with the most delicious fillet of Alaskan salmon. If the instrumentalist is as skilled and dedicated as the chef, and the dining room allows one both to watch and to listen to the performer, I can think of no better recommendation for a restaurant than to recall such an experience to friends afterward. If you are able to arrange for such music in your restaurant, be sure to plan for proper acoustics and positioning of the musician's equipment and seat, with perhaps a small raised platform and a spotlight. In a small place, stringed instruments should be acoustic, rather than electronically amplified. Set your prices to allow you to pay a fair fee to the musician; provide a receptacle for tips discreetly placed near the performer or near the cashier (plainly marked as to its purpose); and be certain to give the performer's name a prominent position in the restaurant and in your advertising.

The function of a restaurant and its management is simply this: to make people feel better when they leave than they did when they arrived.

For all this, you must make sure the performance meets the same standards set for other music, particularly with regard to loudness. Not all of your patrons will want to take their attention away from each other and their meals to listen to, or be quiet for, even the most accomplished live performer. Both you and the musician must understand and accept that. Also, the business of serving meals must go on through it all. One disadvantage to having live performers on a busy night is that table turnover may be affected by diners who linger over wine or coffee to hear one more set. It may be necessary, in a small restaurant, to schedule live performers after the main dinner hours or at other off-peak times.

Dinner Theater

Combining food service with theatrical performances is not a new idea. With the growth and popularity of smaller, more intimate theater settings, and with versatile repertory companies performing theater-in-the-round and improvisational theater, you may be considering the idea of serving more than a snack, desserts, and drinks in a theater-restaurant format. But this presents special seating and table placement problems.

Most informal theater settings I have seen are theaters first and dining rooms despite themselves. In most cases where the meal service is best carried out, the building was originally designed for another use than a theater. (The hotel nightclubs still flourishing in meccas of dubious distinction such as Las Vegas work very well, but not as small restaurants.) Many dinner theaters that were converted from regular theaters suffer from awkwardness in service as well as from menu limitations because of inadequate kitchen facilities. Often the eating surface hardly qualifies as a table, and the inability of the server to move directly from the kitchen to the customer is annoying because he must constantly pass by the other diners in the row. The remedy for this is to remove several seats in each row to improve accessibility. But the economics of theater operation are so precarious that removing 10 or 20 percent of the seats is not feasible. Setting up temporary aisles for the dinner service is a more likely solution, but it assumes that your theater does not have fixed rows of attached seats.

If your dining room was not previously a theater, you can avoid the problem of too many tiers for your tables and make the servers' task safer and less tiring. By using a raised platform for the stage, you can perhaps eliminate tiers entirely except for the outermost edge of the room farthest from the performers. Naturally, your chairs must be comfortable for the duration of both the dinner and the show, which could total three or four hours.

One way to break up this period, and to solve the seating capacity problem at the same time, is to plan a short break after the dinner hour and to encourage the audience to gather in a lounge or even an outdoor patio where after-dinner drinks are served while your crew rearranges the dining room into a theater. This requires that the patrons finish their meal by the prescribed hour, but it does also allow theater-goers who do not wish to eat out to gather before curtain time. You cannot hope to fill the auditorium with dinner patrons, although if you keep the tables set up the theater-only customers who arrive early are more likely to have a drink, especially if you do not have bar service or a lounge.

The speed and efficiency with which dinner is prepared and served is a critical factor in how well you can hold the entire affair down to a reasonable duration. Some theater-goers do have to pay babysitters too. Any setup that requires the removal and replacement of seats and tables is generally an impractical use of people's energy and storage space inside the theater.

One dinner-theater arrangement avoids the entire problem of food service in the theater by serving the meal first in a dining room that is connected to the theater but separated entirely from the stage area. Thus, the dinner setting can be a lovely restaurant with a charming ambiance and an interesting bill of fare. The single-price dinner-theater ticket includes a choice of several regular dinner entrées at a price below what the dinner would otherwise cost if one subtracted the full price of the theater ticket. There is an entrance to the theater directly from the dining room, but theater patrons who do not wish to eat are undisturbed by last-minute clearing of food service paraphernalia. At the same time, the restaurant can continue to operate independently, both during the showtimes and when nothing at all is going on in the theater. This arrangement seems to me an excellent solution to all the difficulties presented by dinner theater.

How Some Others Have Done It

The restaurants described below are examples of what others have actually done to solve a major problem of location, remodeling, or aptness of style for the premises. They are quite different kinds of places, but they all reflect some common characteristics. They are the unique expressions of their founders' individual styles and approaches to food service. Each is comfortable in terms of friendliness and concern for the patrons, with taste and décor appropriate to the locale. They also share an enviable reputation for excellence. The different owners are alike in that none is likely to do what others have already done; rather, each will do precisely what he or she believes strongly in. It is not surprising that the result is uncompromising high quality, uniqueness, customer and critical acclaim, and financial success.

The Hamlet: Converting an Abandoned Building

The health inspector said it couldn't be done. But Norm and Maggie Hamlet of Los Angeles and Cambria, California, were convinced that the location for their small Armenian-style restaurant in Harmony, California (population 18), was feasible. No matter that the old Harmony Valley Creamery Association building was hardly a building at all anymore, especially the shed-like structure that would become their dining room. It was the proposed kitchen area that the inspector had vetoed.

Norm insisted on knowing what requirements they had to meet and explained to the inspector how they would construct a "building within a building" to satisfy all the codes. And so they did. The Hamlets negotiated a five-year lease for the restaurant space, with an option to renew for another five years. They paid for all the remodeling, but much of the actual work was done by the owner of the building and by the Hamlets themselves. Building permits were originally applied for in 1974, but delays, red tape, and slow construction prevented completion of the work until May 1975, when the Hamlet restaurant opened as the main attraction in a collection of small artisans' shops.

Within a few months the Hamlet had attracted loyal customers and critical acclaim for its food, décor, and friendly atmosphere. The dining room combined authentic weathered wood with the freshness of flowers and crisp blue linens. Despite the limitations of the tiny kitchen and storage spaces, on a busy night four to five times the population of Harmony was served at the ten tables of the Hamlet.

The restaurant, though successful, eventually moved to a new location for a variety of reasons. Tiny Harmony is located on California's foggy coastal Route 1 north of Morro Bay, in an area most heavily traveled during the summer by people heading for the Hearst Castle at San Simeon or points north on the scenic highway leading to Big Sur and the Carmel-Monterey peninsula. In 1977, a new owner took over the Harmony property and differences arose between the new landlord and the Hamlets. The restaurateurs were also suffering from the effects of an exhausting schedule of lunch and dinner service and from their space limitations. Just after the Memorial Day weekend in 1978, the Hamlet restaurant in Harmony closed. The remaining time on the lease, as well as the furniture, fixtures, and décor, were sold to the new landlord.

The Hamlet was relocated in a newly constructed adjunct to a two-year-old motel on a highway frontage road just south of the Hearst Castle State Historical Monument in San Simeon, which is visited each year by more than two million people. These more spacious and practical quarters offered the possibilities of improving the kitchen design and expanding the dining room capacity, while keeping the character of a small restaurant with closely controlled quality. The ultimate effect of the move was to relocate an excellent operation to a more favorable venue. The restaurant was not reopened until mid-July, missing nearly half of the summer season while final work was done on the building. Some old customers were lost through a combination of an inflation-induced rise in prices and the added distance for the established clientele to reach the new location. Nevertheless, the potential for good patronage was realized. Persistence and maintenance of the fine, friendly dining experience at the Hamlet overcame the effects of uprooting an established business with an excellent reputation.

The process was repeated when a unique property became available just a few years later. The Exotic Gardens on Highway 1 at the intersection of Moonstone Beach Drive was a very specialized nursery of cacti, succulents, palms, and evergreens, with a magnificent view of the Pacific Ocean to the west and the gardens to the east. Completed in 1982, the present restaurant building has two levels, with the upper level housing the main dining room, a small dance floor, and a large bar affording an unrestricted view of the ocean. The lower level, which was the initial dining area before completion of the second floor, now houses a large wine cellar and a serving facility that also works well for weddings and other private functions. Regular live performance music events, dubbed "At the Hamlet," include the Famous Jazz Artist Series. Just outside, surrounded by the gardens, is a pleasant outdoor table service area, where full meal service during the best weather days is enjoyed on the leeward side of the building. Under the able ownership of Roy Ford, a partner in the second location, the Hamlet at Moonstone Gardens is in its second quarter-century of successful operation just north of Cambria, California. Norm Hamlet, the surviving founder, enjoys a well-deserved retirement, his legacy a testament to his hard work, love of good food and music, and sense of style.

The Sea Chest: Another Conversion

In 1959, Walter Cole, a long-time West Coast sailor, boatyard operator, and newly relocated rancher, decided to sell his large collection of nautical items by opening a shop on Highway 1 leading to the Hearst Castle. He purchased a two-story building right across from the Pacific Ocean, remodeled it with nautical themes, and named the store the Sea Chest. Shortly thereafter, Highway 1 was relocated eastward to widen and improve the roadway, and the bypassed section along the coast was renamed Moonstone Beach Drive. Two years later, when asked by a gentleman from southern California whether he knew of any ocean-front property for sale, Walt offered the place to the man, who immediately accepted and wrote out a deposit check, despite the buyer's wife's cautionary comment, "Are you sure you know what you are doing?" His reply, "Yes, I know," reflected what his son, Jim Clarke, remembers as his simple desire to own land close to the ocean. The Sea Chest could not be any closer, and for the next 11 years, the Clarke family would come up from the Pomona area, where they operated concession stands selling hot dogs and soda to attendees at sporting events. In Cambria, they could enjoy the beauty of the isolated beach and the funky old building.

In 1973, Jim and his wife, Karen, moved to the site and began work building a home behind the existing building and remodeling the Sea

Chest to open a seafood restaurant. The work was completed two years later, and in July 1975, the restaurant opened to the great satisfaction and pleasure of locals and tourists who had found the place and filled it to capacity on the first night.

Jim saw no reason to change the name since there was already a nice sign on the building. The rest, as they say, is history. At that time, there were few real restaurants in Cambria, and none were limited to fresh seafood in a dinner setting. The nearest competition was 20 miles to the south, in Morro Bay, but none featured a view of an unspoiled beach where driftwood, moonstones, and jade nuggets were still to be found.

Jim's remodel of the interior incorporated an open bar where raw oysters and all the broiling could be seen from the counter seating. All dining room table and counter seating is on a first-come basis and neither reservations nor credit cards are accepted. But there are board games and cards available for adults and children in the waiting area, where drinks are served while one waits. These days, despite the dinner hour having been moved forward from 5:30 to 5:00 P.M., the line for entry forms as early as 4:00 P.M., six days a week.

In the years since their first success, few changes have been made to the menu. Abalone is no longer available. Some expansion of the dining area and on-site parking has been accomplished without changing the essential character of the site. Not so for the surrounding land, however, as the Sea Chest is now surrounded by numerous motels and tourist cottages and the area now features restaurants galore, but none can match the ambiance, authenticity, and openly prepared fresh seafood bill-of-fare that visitors and locals dream about once they have eaten at the Sea Chest.

Jim's presence in or near the dining room over the past 30 years of operation has ensured the consistent quality of the food as well as a welcoming feeling imparted to all guests. But the Sea Chest managers, cooks, and wait staff, trained to carry out the standards originally set, are now the mainstay of its enduring reputation and success. Most have worked there for many, many years. The smooth operation allows Jim the leisure to travel and enjoy favorite pastimes. Its location and quality have allowed the Sea Chest to play a significant role, along with Hearst Castle and the magnificent coastline, in attracting millions of visitors to the area.

The Jasmine Café: *Haute Cuisine in a Historic Setting*

The planned community called Reston lies among the rolling hills and runs (creeks) of Fairfax County, Virginia. Robert E. Simon bought most of the property that was the site of a bourbon distillery and surrounding cornfields, using the proceeds from his sale of New York City's Carnegie Hall. In the early 1960s, his vision of a new town where people could live, work, and play among trees, lakes, and pathways and incorporating all types of housing became a reality, with its first man-made lake, Anne, and a town center plaza at the lake's north end.

Washington Plaza at Lake Anne features a high-rise apartment building dubbed Heron House, a church, nearby parking, and clusters of combination retail stores on the ground level with condominium dwellings on the upper levels. Most of the rest of the lake shore is lined with apartment condominiums, townhouses, and single-family dwellings, many of which have docks and electric-powered floating patios used in summer to motor up to the plaza. If the occupants are not dining on their own, they may very well be on their way to the Jasmine Café, just beyond the fountain on the plaza.

In 1988, after nearly 10 years of plying his craft in various upscale establishments, chef Eduardo Faubert came to Reston and opened his own restaurant, named for his wife. A 1979 graduate of the Cornell University School of Hotel Management, Eduardo well understood both the risks and the advantages of opening a small place located far away from the passing traffic on well-known thoroughfares. But he wanted the power to control his own culinary destiny in a place where his family could prosper and his children could attend excellent schools. He prepared a formal business plan based on a thorough demographic analysis of the market area from which he could expect to draw lunch and dinner guests. He factored in relevant intangibles, such as the fact that the prospective location had been the site of previous restaurants, the most recent having had success and profitability serving Thai food. Chef Faubert credits his business plan as the main reason he received the necessary bank loan to purchase the property.

The Jasmine Café has an eclectic but limited menu with a daily special soup, individual pizza, chef's selection, seafood special, and dessert offered in addition to the seasonal menu. The basic menu changes seasonally four times a year. There is a small L-shaped bar that is a favorite of locals who are weekly and even daily regulars. It also makes dining alone a friendlier experience when the servers have time to interact as they work. The walls feature local artwork that changes periodically, exhibiting the efforts of Reston artists, many of whom study and work at the Art Center nearby. Service at outdoor tables on the plaza under umbrella shades is one of the most popular features enjoyed during the mild Virginia seasons.

Other plaza neighbors include a book shop; a pharmacy; the Reston Museum; two coffee shops; several other restaurants also serving lunch, dinner, and Sunday brunch; plus various other services such as hair and nail salons, barbershops, dry cleaning and alterations, jewelry sales and repair, and the like. The other restaurants also serve at outdoor tables under umbrella coverings, which gives the whole plaza the feel of a European venue, with the view of the lake and pedestrian traffic strolling by, that is rare in this part of the country. One of the regular patrons, as of this writing, is none other than Robert E. Simon, a resident of Heron House.

In 2002, the space adjacent to the original Jasmine Café dining room became available. The demand for tables during inclement weather as well as the chance to serve special events such as wedding rehearsal dinners, anniversary celebrations, and business holiday parties made the expansion feasible and desirable. The new space opened to the delight of the locals, who cherish this island of excellence where Chef Faubert is sometimes seen in his toque and whites, chatting with both new and longtime diners. But even when he is not present, the output from his kitchen is indistinguishable from his own product, befitting the master chef who designs and guides every step of preparation during the training process. The training of his kitchen staff, who are El Salvadoran immigrants, is aided immeasurably by Eduardo's fluency in several languages, including Spanish. But the language connection is surpassed by the clear feeling that the chef is the mentor in a process that will bring long-term benefits to the trainee. The end result can best be described as loyalty—to the chef and his business; to the quality and consistency of the food presented to the customer; and finally *from* the chef to the trainee, as his performance improves and succeeds.

The Jasmine Café does only minimal advertising, although the initial opening period and later expansion generated a local news buzz. The soon-to-be-established Web site will provide information and directions to new customers. Chef Faubert has no need for an in-house computer system for such a small kitchen and about 30 indoor tables. There is just room for the credit card authenticator behind the bar. As is common at many such places, his staff has been working with him for many years and the routine works smoothly, seemingly effortlessly. This reliability of service and the combination of a regular menu of favorites for the season plus innovative special dishes, such as Virginia peanut soup, have made the Jasmine Café one of the favorite restaurants in the Washington, D.C., region, despite its somewhat off-the-beaten-path location. Many Restonians, including Bob Simon (and me), are especially grateful to be able to walk to such a wonderful restaurant whenever the urge arises.

Lake Forest Café: A Place This Book Helped Launch

Barbara Rubin already knew during her college days that she could prepare food to meet her own taste and high standards. While cooking for her roommates, from whom she collected monetary contributions at the beginning of the month, the game was not to serve the same dinner more than once. Using her ability to correct to her own taste the menu items she sampled when dining out, she tested and perfected her recipes during those years. She entered her pies, cakes, and cookies in the local county fairs, taking away many a blue ribbon.

A few years later, after her former college roommate gave her a copy of the first edition of this book, Barbara was inspired to open her own restaurant in 1982. She chose to locate in the historic town of Folsom, California, a suburb east of the capital, Sacramento. She credits the encouragement she gained from the book with giving her the confidence to operate the Lake Forest Café, which serves breakfast and lunch featuring her made-from-scratch recipes. She limits her service to morning and midday meals to try to keep late afternoons and evenings free to raise her family. Her husband has contributed some tailored business forms and report applications that she uses on her computer at home to track performance and trends, but the restaurant eschews any automated systems. If the power fails on a dark morning, the restaurant's staff can carry on with flashlights and candles, cooking with gas to be ready to open on time.

Folsom is an historic gold rush mining locale, and the café is located on the main road connecting Highway 50 to the town center. But these days, loyal customers gained during the past 23 years would go anywhere to find Barbara's homemade blintzes, 43 choices of omelets, three kinds of pancakes, and Mike's Potatoes—named in honor of Barbara's dad, who decried the use of anything but a fresh potato. Barbara even serves a traditional Jewish breakfast dish rarely found in a restaurant, known as matzo-brei, made from matzo and egg. Lunch features six kinds of burgers, 16 different sandwiches, crepe dishes, and quiches, all made on the premises from the best quality ingredients.

The consistent food quality that the kitchen staff has maintained under Barbara's strict supervision and training has won the highest four-star ratings for food and atmosphere from the *Sacramento Bee* newspaper, an accolade rarely awarded to a restaurant that does not serve dinner. *Sacramento Magazine* has featured the Lake Forest Café in its pages. With seating for 48 patrons among only 14 tables, the café truly qualifies as a small restaurant. Service begins at 7:00 A.M. and ends at 1:45 P.M., Wednesday through Sunday. Reservations are taken only for parties of 5 to 10 persons, but with the clear understanding that lateness or no-shows will not be tolerated. Most customers are local, and the line for first-come, first-serve seating is sometimes long. It often includes government officials and local celebrities.

Barbara favors the work ethic of more experienced, mature workers, and her customers benefit from their depth of wisdom. But she also likes to train younger staff before they have become too spoiled by the culture, so she hires and trains staff as young as 14, but limits their shifts to no more than five hours to counteract fatigue. The result is a staff that is both willing and able to maintain her strict standards of food and service. That Barbara Rubin had first used, and continues to use, this book as an inspiration is indeed a singular satisfaction for me, as Barbara personifies precisely why I wrote the book in the first place.

Splash Café: A Wave of the Future?

Pismo Beach on the California Central Coast of San Luis Obispo County has attracted seafood eaters for literally 9,000 years or more.

The Native American Chumash people left evidence of their annual sojourns in the region. In fact, *pismoo* is the Chumash word for tar, which oozes up and washes ashore from offshore oil deposits. The Chumash used pismoo to seal basketry for holding liquids.

There is a new development that bodes well for the future, if Tod Murphy has his way. Barre, Vermont, is the site of Tod's brainchild, an eating establishment whose main purpose is to excel by featuring locally grown food. The Farmers Diner, created in 2002, has already achieved two fundamental objectives; it reached its business plan break-even point of $1,500 gross sales per day in its first year, and it increased its use of local food products from an initial 60 percent to a 70 percent level. But the really exciting part of the story is that Tod, himself a farmer, was able to raise the capital to create a local meat-processing operation. This became necessary when he discovered that the hogs he had arranged to be raised locally would have to be sent afar for slaughter and to make the bacon, ham, and pork he needed for the diner. Such a restaurant business model, if expanded to areas that still have local growers who survived the trends of the past 50 years in America, may prove to be a practical way for socially conscious patrons and investors to take back food production from corporate agribusiness. The nation has paid a huge price for its focus on artificial flavors, shelf-life enhancers, and transportability instead of natural taste, freshness, and the local economy. If Tod writes a book someday (when he finds the time), he could call it *Starting a Small Restaurant Revolution.*

Like the Chumash, the famous Pismo clam is now rarely found. Today, visitors savor the popular meals to be had, featuring Washington State clams and New York steamer clams, at Joanne and Ross Currie's famous Splash Café on Pomeroy Street leading to the beach. Joanne and Ross acquired the original Splash Café in 1991, less than two years after it opened with a limited menu, from the inexperienced (and exhausted) founders.

The new owners expanded and improved the menu, which caters to pedestrian traffic in an informal setting. They also expanded the amount of table and counter seating. At the height of the summer season, the customers assemble in a block-long waiting line of eager eaters.

The café's format is called "half-service," in which customers place their orders at the front counter giving their names to identify their orders. When ready, the food, such as a famous clam chowder served in a hollowed-out round loaf of sourdough bread, is delivered to the seats chosen by the customer, who answers the call. Freshness and quality are easily maintained as a result of the high turnover of customers in this resort setting, and the local climate affords a nearly year-round season for visitors. The city of Pismo Beach schedules visitor events of all sorts virtually all year.

The menu is served daily from 10:00 A.M. to closing time, which can vary with the demand. In addition to seafood items, the café serves a variety of sandwiches and typical salads and side dishes expected by beach-goers. Food is served in disposable paper liners and paper "boats." Utensils are also disposable and beverages are self-poured from a dispensing unit using a cup received at the time the order is placed. Many orders are packaged "to go." Ross is gratified by all the evidence of customer satisfaction, although he worries about recent trends in the public's display of impatient behavior. He notices poor role models for children who witness their parents' rudeness, all of which he attributes to the stressful pace of our daily lives at home and in heavy traffic. Vacations are supposed to be fun, at a slower pace.

Joanne, who has worked in food service since her high school days and has a degree in business and accounting, has not only practiced accountancy, specializing in food service, but has also designed, programmed, installed, and debugged early computer systems tailored for restaurants. She finds no practical advantage for the Splash Café operation to justify installing any in-house systems, since she can keep track of all the important measures on her home computer. The café's "clothesline," a couple of tightly strung wire cables fitted with spring-loaded wooden clothespins to hold each order sheet, carries individual orders back to the kitchen when the clothespin is sent speeding down the line. The café does, however, have a colorful animated Web site at www.splashcafe.com that gets updated periodically. It serves several purposes useful to future and past visitors. As a tourist information source, it covers both the café as well as other attractions to be found in Pismo Beach. It highlights some historical facts of interest and is easy to navigate. Customers can comment to management via the site. But it also enables lovers of Splash Café's famous clam chowder to have a frozen order of the chowder, with or without the sourdough loaf, shipped to them anywhere by air. Not surprisingly, requests for the recipe have come from both *Gourmet* and *Bon Appétit* magazines. More than 10,000 gallons of this rich delicacy are enjoyed by patrons each year.

As this is being written, an exciting new venture is underway to open a second location that will bear the name Splash Café Artisan Bakery. In the nearby city of San Luis Obispo, a few short blocks from the public high school, a former hamburger joint with on-site parking stood at the corner of Monterey Street and California Avenue. The site is less than a mile from the California Polytechnic University campus, where Joanne's brother, Professor Thomas Neuhaus, teaches food science and nutrition. Tom is also an accomplished chef and former restaurateur.

As a way both to educate his students and to make the university a more visible part of the San Luis Obispo business community, Tom several years ago initiated a line of Cal Poly chocolate-covered treats made entirely by students in Tom's kitchen and lab facilities. The chocolate-covered dried fruits, baked goods, and the like are packaged individually and sold at many local retail outlets. Proceeds benefit the Food Science Department's courses and activities. Joanne and Ross are combining their talents and experience with those of Tom and his wife, Eve, to build the new venture.

The existing structure was demolished and a new two-story building has replaced it on the same footprint. The new building houses the Splash Café Artisan Bakery retail counter on the ground level. The second level is home to the chocolate factory, where all the equipment needed for the manufacture of high-quality chocolate and baked goods operates. This combination of activities serves several objectives, in addition to bringing the Splash Café's upgraded menu to a modified but still informal setting typical of a college town. Many deep-fried dishes have been dropped from the original menu in favor of more popular broiled fish, such as ahi tuna and salmon, served on salad or in tacos. The ever-popular calamari and fish and chips have been retained. The service has reduced the use of disposables by employing reusable plastic boat holders. Takeout represents a significant portion of the patronage, especially when schools are in session. The high school students are permitted to leave the campus for lunch, and both Cal Poly and commuter traffic passes by, en route to campus or to the on-ramp for the main highway headed north to bedroom communities.

But the most interesting objective relates to the ancillary businesses. This complex affords the Cal Poly food science students who merit employment at one of the three businesses a real-world work experience under the tutelage of expert management. They are exposed to a variety of food production and service roles and have to deal directly with the stresses and limitations of a small business as well as the general public. Eve Neuhaus, herself an outstanding educator, artist, and humanist, brings an added dimension to the partnership that rounds out the management team needed to operate an enterprise in two locations. The plan reflects a logical application of the combined talents and reputations of the owners, the needs of the community and the students, and the fortuitous location. What could be more exciting?

Dining Room Practice

RESTAURANT IS THEATER. If you view your dining room operation from this perspective, you will work from the right starting point. From the moment the customers first make contact with the players—whether this is on the telephone, in person, or even by letter—the tone of the response they get is essential to their dining pleasure. As in theater, both the voice and the body must convey your message. The message a small restaurant gives is friendship, calm and graceful service, and artfully prepared food of the highest quality. The mood and demeanor of the dining room staff bespeak this message in the subtlest ways.

Everyone who answers the telephone at your restaurant should be trained to use a pleasant, well-modulated voice. The opening phrase should be "Good morning [afternoon, evening]," followed by the name of the restaurant. You can check on how well it is done by calling your place at different times.

Whether your show is just a little "one-act" breakfast or lunch stop, an "improvisational" buffet restaurant, or a "grand opera" dinner house complete with curtain calls by the chef after the final act, it will follow certain basic and logical sequences intended to please the audience and ensure smooth timing of the performance. The following synopsis of restaurant scenes describes dinner in a typical "three-act" table-service establishment. With some additions or deletions, it applies as well to the service of other meals or to variants of the table-service restaurant. It should establish a framework on which to build an understanding of the specific topics discussed in detail in this and subsequent chapters.

Before the Show

On Stage

- The servers arrive early enough to check and fill all dispensers of condiments, relishes, beverages, salad bins, ice, water, linens, silverware, and so on. Tables are set, menus and "specials" are noted, and wine lists are reviewed.

- The host, maitre d', or captain checks reservations; prepares for large parties that will require moving of tables; checks dining room temperature and lighting and restroom conditions and supplies; and double checks on the preparations of servers and buspersons, especially the initial setup of tables and serving stations. Candles or table lights and flowers are checked and replenished, if needed. Just before opening, the dining room floor and seats are scrutinized for hazards, debris, or water.

- The manager and chef give last-minute instructions for

Backstage

- The chef and kitchen personnel have prepared any foods whose cooking time needed to begin before opening. Backup amounts for service later in the evening are in preparation. For dishes that are prepared to order, setup is made for ease of continuous operations during the mealtime. Extra salad and dressings are made ready; vegetables and garnishes are presliced; and cuts of meat or seafood are prepared and trimmed based on the number of reservations and anticipated business for the meal to come. Ovens and steam tables are prepared for use.

- The dishwasher stacks clean plates where the chef can easily get to them for meal assembly. The dish room is cleaned up from washing the prep utensils, and bus trays and carts are wiped clean in readiness for dining room dishes. Bins for dirty linens, trash, bottles, and garbage are emptied. The dishwashing ma-

handling specific parties and on how to describe the ingredients and preparation of special dishes or sauces for that night. Any regular items in short supply are discussed and hints for promoting fresh items or special desserts that might spoil if kept beyond that day are suggested, especially if it is the night before a day the restaurant is normally closed.

- If server rotation or table stations are not already assigned, they are now clearly established. Note is taken of any servers who are scheduled to arrive after the start of the serving to handle the busiest hours, and any who are scheduled to depart early are so reminded. New employees are reminded about important procedures and the handling of tips.

- Outside signs and lights are checked, if necessary.

chine is checked for proper water temperatures.

- The servers set up plates, utensils, and supplies for any items they normally assemble and serve, such as salads, soups, desserts, butter, relish, crackers, bread sticks, hot bread or rolls, house wines, and side orders.

- The refrigerator stocks are checked for items regularly dispensed, such as drinks and special condiments for that meal. Backup stocks in the storeroom or cooler are also checked to ensure replenishment of reach-in refrigerators.

- The chef gives last-minute instructions to the host or maitre d' and the servers about any important changes in the menu, routine, or timing to accommodate the night's menu or the state of readiness in the kitchen.

- Sometimes staff meals are served before the start of the dinner hour. This is not usual practice for servers, but it is common for dishwashers.

When the Curtain Rises

On Stage

- After taking care of coats, the host seats the diners. The host or another staff member offers the menu and wine list. Special menu items are announced; regrets are expressed for any items that are no longer available. Often the server's name is announced at the table.

- The server acknowledges the party's presence and arrives as soon as practical to take drink orders. Sufficient time is allowed for diners to study the menu. Bread, water, and whatever else is served early are delivered to the table.

- At the right moment, according to the diners' wishes and your custom, the food order and dinner wine order are taken. For large parties or unusual requests, the server notes carefully the seating arrangement and sequence of the orders taken. Often for very large parties, more than one server takes orders, with the group split up in a logical way. Even if this is not done, a large party is usually served the hot food by more than one server. If separate checks are allowed for large groups, the server arranges for it in advance of taking orders.

Backstage

- According to the established kitchen practice, the server delivers the order ticket to the chef, often accompanied by a verbal announcement ("Order!"), especially when the chef is not at his usual station. The server carefully notes which parts of the order he or she must prepare or assemble (such as different salad dressings and beverages) and the proper timing for each. Any special instructions to the chef or variations requested by the diner are noted plainly on the order ticket and also are usually pointed out verbally at the time the ticket is turned in.

- If the responsibility for taking orders for drinks and serving them does not lie with the regular server, the necessary coordination of service and tallying the price on the order or dinner check is arranged between the staff involved.

- According to your kitchen practice, early courses such as soup and salad are assembled either by the server, by kitchen assistants, or by both for each table.

- Supplies of hot bread, rolls, or other side dishes served from the kitchen are kept at a level

- Early courses are served without interfering with apéritifs or before-meal wines. Dirty dishes from the preceding course are always removed before serving the next course. Any untouched plate of food must be noted by the server, who is on the alert for something amiss. Whatever course immediately precedes the main dish (usually it's salad) is carefully watched for completion so that it may be removed or set to the side to allow service of the hot main course as soon as it is ready.

- When the main dish has been at the table for one or two minutes, the server returns to ask if all is well and whether any last-minute requests can be filled.

sufficient to serve the number of diners out front.

- The buspersons apprise the servers and chef of the progress of clearing early course plates from each table to ensure timely serving of the next course.

- The chef looks at the main course orders for that table and mentally notes the required cooking time for each order so the diners in that group can be served all at the same time. When the server later signals that the course before the entrée has been served, the chef starts that table's orders, if possible. On nights when time permits it, the chef often will ask to be told about slow eaters so as to avoid rushing them.

- The warm plates are set up for assembly of the meal and the dinner items are artfully arranged to make an attractive and appetizing array with the garnishes and any special side condiments. At the right time during this assembly, the server is signaled for pickup.

- The server appears to pick up the order just as the last plate is being finished (for large parties, the last plate the server can carry at one time). The server always checks the order ticket before taking the plates; any errors are corrected

- Servers and buspersons are on the alert throughout the meal to anticipate the need for more bread, rolls, butter, wine or other drink, cream, coffee, tea, water, or other such requests, and to provide assistance with spills or other mishaps, especially when there are small children present.

- When the diners are obviously finished with the main course, the plates are removed, and the server reappears to take the dessert orders. The dessert is announced and served, along with any other last courses, such as fruit and cheese, coffee, tea, after-dinner wines, or whatever.

- The dinner check is not tallied until it is reasonably certain that the diners' wants have been fully satisfied. If it is your custom not to present the check until it is requested, be sure the customer is aware of that. Large party checks are reviewed for arithmetic errors or omissions by a second person before they are presented to the table. (This is a good practice for all checks, if time permits.)

- Your policy on personal checks and credit cards may be discussed when the check is presented. If the diner is expected to make payment to a cashier,

quickly. The plates are taken up so the ladies at the table are the first to be served (eldest first), except when the far side of the table is difficult to reach; those seated on that side, male or female, are served first. Meat entrées that have been cooked to order (rare, medium, well-done, or gradations thereof) are identified to the server for proper delivery at the table.

- Whenever possible, everything that can be done to anticipate the chef's next need—whether for plates, utensils, or components of the meal being assembled—is done by those assisting the chef. All spills are immediately wiped away to avoid accidents, staining, or burns to the server or the diner. Plates with hot food are not overfilled for the same reason.

that fact must be made clear
as well.

- When the server, the host, or
the manager handles a credit
card payment or returns
change and the receipt for a
cash transaction, the guests are
thanked and asked to com-
ment on the restaurant or to
recommend it to friends. This
can also take place when coats
are returned or the guest book
is signed.

- As soon as the party leaves the
table, any dirty plates, glasses,
silverware, and other remnants
of the meal are quietly removed by using some type of
tray or bus container. Depending on your custom, the server,
the busperson, or the host
takes care to remove the tip, if
it was left in cash on the table.
The table and the area around
it are examined for articles that
may have been dropped or forgotten by the diners, so they
may be returned before the patrons have left the restaurant.

- The empty table and the floor
are checked for spills and food
particles and the table is reset
using a clean cloth, if necessary. It is set for the exact
number in the party awaiting
that table; otherwise, it is set
for whatever number is practical. Toward the end of the
mealtime, vacated tables often
are not reset or are reset for the
next mealtime, when tableware settings will be different.

- The dirty dishes, tableware,
and linens from the dining
room are delivered directly to
the dish room, never near
the area where food is being
prepared or meals assembled.
Whenever possible, kitchen
personnel assist servers
whose orders are waiting for
pickup by taking dirty dishes
from them so the servers can
proceed directly to the
pickup upon entering the
kitchen. The dishwasher fa-
cilitates deposit of dirty
dishes by keeping the dish
room free of spills or tall
stacks of dishes in or near the
repository for dirty tableware, and by making available an empty bin or other
area that the server or busperson can reach without
bending down. The busper-
sons assist in this during the
busiest times by holding
dirty dishes in the dining
room or other places, so long
as the tables are cleared as
quickly as needed.

- The chef must first be con-
sulted about any requests
from diners to give compli-
ments in person to the chef
or to enter the kitchen area
for any reason whatsoever.

After Curtain Calls

On Stage

- The night's receipts are counted by the manager and the dinner checks totaled. Tips that were included on credit card drafts can be paid in cash to the servers, if that is your practice. At the same time, the checks are reviewed for errors in prices charged and for items that were served but omitted from the check. Errors are discussed with the servers, especially those in training, either that same evening or the next day.

- The dining room is cleaned to remove food particles and the remains of spills. Salt, pepper, and sweetener holders are carefully wiped clean of food residues and are refilled for the next mealtime. Depending on your custom, tables are set for the next meal service or wiped clean and prepared for the next crew to set them up.

- The restrooms are thoroughly cleaned and supplies replenished.

- Music equipment is prepared for the next day's use and turned off.

- The windows and doors are closed and locked and any alarms for smoke or burglary detection are set. Air condi-

Backstage

- The crew is served whatever meals you customarily serve. The cleanup crew begins work on the kitchen as soon as possible after the food is put away. The servers and kitchen assistants complete their side-work chores and replenish supplies.

- All usable leftovers are placed in tightly covered containers with as little room for air as possible. Perishable food and supplies are returned quickly to the refrigerators and coolers. The chef decides what use may be made of leftovers for the next day's specials for lunch or dinner. Notes are written for the early morning cooks, giving important instructions about use of leftovers, deliveries of supplies, or other matters not part of the routine.

- The cleanup crew takes apart the steam table and all food-processing equipment, such as slicers, and puts parts that touch the food directly through the dishwasher or disinfectant, while wiping down the rest of the equipment. The stove, griddle, grill, and microwave ovens receive special attention in the cleanup. Usually, the food preparation areas in which servers have done their work are wiped clean by

tioning, fans, and heating units are turned off.

• Unnecessary inside lights are turned off or dimmed. Outside lights or lighted signs are turned off if not on a timer.

• The sign is changed to "closed."

the servers before they depart, as are the coffeemaker and milk dispenser. The cleanup crew double checks these areas. The floor is swept and mopped clean each night.

• The dishwasher completes his chores: he puts away all dishware, glassware, and tableware; scours all the pots; and cleans and rinses away all food particles in and around the dishwashing machine and drainboards. The machine is turned off and the tank drained (make sure the heater is off). Walls around the dish room are wiped down.

• All garbage, empty bottles, and other disposables are removed from the kitchen area to whatever outdoor or enclosed place is available.

• The closing security checklist is followed for turning off ovens, steam tables, other heating elements, fans, and lights. Storeroom locks are checked, as are the windows and doors to the kitchen.

Reservations

"No one will be seated after curtain time." In a small restaurant, "curtain time" for a table on a busy night is the time reserved. If you take reservations, do not hold them for more than a few minutes when someone else is waiting for a table. Tell callers when you accept their reservation how long it will be held on a busy night.

Scheduling Table Use

When scheduling reservations, how long do you figure a table will be occupied by one party? This is determined by several factors, including the number of courses in the meal, the number of tables the server must take care of, the speed and coordination in the kitchen, and whether you serve wine and desserts. There are a few other minor factors whose influence is subtle—the hardness of the seat, the temperature of the room, the proximity of the restaurant to another attraction such as a theater, and even whether the waiting room full of people can be seen by those still at their tables. The range of occupancy time for planning optimum table use is from about one hour per party to as long as one and three-quarters hours. If someone lingers for more than that and you need the table, you are in trouble.

If your meals are long affairs, you will have to have more tables or higher prices, or both, to make up for the loss of turnover. You may even choose to have only two seatings per night and to fill up twice by reservation only. This is practical only when your reputation and the demand for your services permit you to limit flexibility.

Simultaneous Seating

Do not hesitate to tell someone requesting a reservation that the time he desires is not convenient but that you will have a table 15 minutes earlier or later. He will usually take it and this device smooths the flow of parties. In a small dining room with only two or three servers, it is not a good idea to have a lot of parties seated all at once. The exception to this rule is at opening time, when it is not so bad.

Spacing the parties by 5 to 15 minutes also improves the work flow in the kitchen. In addition, having a few minutes between seatings gives the servers time to take orders in a systematic manner. If you have a limited amount of any special entrée on the menu for the evening, it is important to be able to notify people as they are seated that the special is gone.

When a time period for dining room use is already booked for all your tables, it is sometimes still possible to squeeze in one more party. Make a note on your reservation sheet whenever a party has arrived and been seated early. Also check the progress at the tables to see whether there are any fast eaters who may not have dessert or coffee. You may be able to feed a hungry family who just found your place by accident and had no time to reserve a table.

"No-Shows"

If you clearly explain that you will not hold reservations for more than five minutes, 99 out of 100 people will understand why you gave away their table when they were late. Of course, the other 1 percent may be like the party of six that reserved a table at our restaurant for 8:00 P.M. on Friday and did not show up. The next night, when we were completely booked up for the evening, the previous night's no-shows appeared at 8:00 P.M. with sheepish grins. Some people will try anything once.

Once upon a time there was a man named Williams, who made a reservation at a small restaurant for a party of 12 on a busy Saturday night. The Williams party never showed up and didn't call to cancel. Ever since then, the maitre d' gets shivers whenever anyone named Williams calls for a reservation.

Especially on busy nights, it is a good rule to give away a table to a waiting party if the one with the reservation does not show up within a few minutes of the appointed time. The exception is for a large party. It always takes a little longer for a large group to get going, so they are often late. Unless you have several large tables available, you should give them 10 to 15 minutes to arrive. More often than not, they will show up. Just hope they don't appear just after you have given their table to a party of two.

Sometimes you get a feeling about whether a particular reservation will be kept. If the caller seems somehow uncertain, be sure to act on your hunch and ask him to telephone you if his plans change. (He may even do so.) Another good candidate for a no-show is the party that simply must have a couple of cocktails before dinner. They show up early for that purpose, assuming you have a bar and are chagrined to find that you serve only beer and wine. When you direct them to the nearest bar, be sure to get their name, so you can call to find out whether they are still there when they fail to arrive for their reserved table. It may not affect you the same way, but I always felt downright insulted when someone didn't show up for a reservation and didn't call to cancel. Those who did call, whatever the stated reason, received our warmest thanks and our sincere hope to serve them some other time.

Greeting Patrons

The front desk host, hostess, maitre d', or owner sets the scene as narrator of your restaurant "play." He also doubles as usher, ticket seller, and supporting character. Before long, this versatile member of the cast will be able to discern in a second or two whether the people who enter are intent on dining or have just stopped by to see what your place is like. During those first few seconds, the potential customer gets a feeling of welcome or indifference, a sense of quality and price, and a desire either to stay or to leave gracefully. Some will say, "We'll be back." Nothing gave me more satisfaction than when, on certain slow evenings, people stopped in to the restaurant because it "looked interesting," perused the menu, asked how long before they could have a table, and then went to check out another nearby restaurant. In four or five minutes they reappeared for a table. Invariably, they said they had returned "because this place smelled great and looked so nice and homey." But it is more than décor or aroma. The feeling of a dining room also depends on the subtle messages that emanate from the people who manage it.

It should be a firm requirement that every member of the staff in the dining room be prepared to give a friendly greeting to customers who enter the restaurant. Whoever notices them first should make eye contact and say something with a smile. If the host or maitre d' is occupied elsewhere at the moment, the greeting should be issued by a server, a busperson, or even by the dishwasher who happens to be there picking up a tray full of dirty dishes. There is something special about being noticed and acknowledged immediately. Seeds of uncertainty are planted in every minute that one is ignored, especially if the staff is scurrying about. It is as if the curtain has gone up on the first act, but all you see are stagehands acting as if the curtain were still closed.

"Watch the Coats"

I never believed that those "watch your coat" signs in coffee shops were really necessary until I became responsible for everyone's coats. The problem of checking coats and hats is not a trivial one, especially in areas where cold winters call for expensive garments like goose-down jackets. Hang coats where they can be watched carefully by either the cashier or the patrons. Expensive raincoats, hats, and favorite garments do get deliberately or accidentally taken. If your clientele are likely to wear expensive outer garments, such as fur or designer coats, you should discuss with your insurance agent your liability in the event of loss. Such garments should not be taken to the table, even if you have a nearby rack to hold them. You should prepare some space that is safe and clear in which to store them temporarily and use a simple coat-check tag to identify each garment, perhaps by table number. Regardless of your legal responsibility, if you have many clients with such tastes, common courtesy demands that you safeguard their garments for the duration of their visit, just as you would if they were guests in your home. If you allow people to keep their wraps at the table, be particularly careful when serving boiled potatoes and beet borscht.

King Vidor, the film director, was an occasional but devoted patron of our restaurant. One day he left his hat on the antique English bentwood hall tree, and forgot it when he departed. When he got home, he called to assure himself that I had his favorite hat, a beautiful old wide-brimmed felt work of the highest quality. I promised to guard it well. But there really was no good place to keep the hat where it would have proper protection, yet be visible to one of our staff in case Mr. Vidor should come for it while I was gone. Finally, I decided to put it in a conspicuous but safe place. At the time, our bubble-top dessert cart was not being used and was kept in the entry room. I placed Mr. Vidor's hat inside it on a napkin. It attracted much comment, especially from those who thought it was a marvelously crafted cake, but those to whom I revealed that it was King Vidor's hat thought me daft.

Server Stations

The routine for assigning tables is designed with one main purpose: to provide the best possible timing for meal service by balancing the load among each server and busperson. Each table in the dining room should be given a number; a chart of the dining room layout should be posted in the kitchen for easy reference by the staff. Some restaurants then establish a fixed "station," or area of tables, to be each server's responsibility. As they arrive, customers are directed by the host to tables in each station in rotation. The only foul-up in the plan occurs when the customer insists on sitting at a table out of rotation sequence, which can temporarily overload one server while another is idle.

Another method that works in a small dining room is to allow the servers to take parties in rotation as they arrive, regardless of table. This can also create an overload, though, if chance causes the larger parties all to fall to one server for several rounds. But a balance can easily be worked out by switching parties, especially if reservations allow some advance planning. The very best service to the customer occurs when astute servers take it upon themselves to respond to anyone else's table at crucial times, such as to take the wine order before the meal or to fulfill a special request.

Most servers view table assignment as a means of ensuring that they all get a fair share of the tips. When an inexperienced server has just started work, however, it is important to limit the number of tables he or she is assigned, in order to give the newcomer time to learn the job well. But the question of tips is not a simple one. If you want to see the preliminaries to a cat fight, just listen to the reaction of other servers to one who grabs too many parties in a rotation system. Not only does this situation cost the other servers some tips, but it usually costs your patrons comfort as well, when they sense the friction between the staff members or are badly served by the overloaded one. You must watch for and prevent such backbiting.

There is a lot to be said for having all servers pool their tips for the shift as a way of defusing pettiness. For this system to work well, the servers must feel that each is doing a fair share of the side work and setup, cleanup, and preparation for the next shift. This can easily be accomplished if all the people make an effort to get along. Pooling tips has the added advantage of making it easier to decide who should be assigned which station or parties. It also diminishes the effect on one server of getting a small tip or getting "stiffed" (no tip). Pooling tips does require that your servers all be of approximately equal skill, so that no one is constantly asking for help from the others.

What Happens at the Table

Menu and Wine List

Your customer has been comfortably seated, coats and hats have been accounted for, and the menu and wine list have been offered. At this point it is imperative that the server for that table acknowledge the diners' presence as soon as possible. If the server cannot approach the table within a reasonably short time, it is still possible for the customer to be reassured by a nod, a smile, or preferably a few words that the server will be with them momentarily. One way of doing this is to deliver a small relish dish or appetizer for them to munch on while they decide what to order.

Typically, the server takes initial drinks orders and places them before the food order is placed. On a busy night, the host or maitre d' might do this to save time. Some restaurants do not have the wine steward or server ask about interest in wine until the dinner has been ordered. I find this an unnecessary and sometimes annoying delay. People are entitled to decide for themselves, in whatever order they choose, whether or not to have wine. The menu and wine list should be presented at the start, when the party is seated. However, because there are some nondrinkers who act offended if wine is offered, be certain to inquire first whether the wine list is of interest to them. (Thank goodness for the many people who would be offended if the wine list were not offered.)

It is more efficient if all your servers are thoroughly familiar with your wine list and with any selections that are not listed. But at dinner time, when the servers must respond promptly to the demands of the kitchen and the patrons, it is important to have someone else available in the dining room who can knowledgeably discuss and recommend wines to your guests. There are more and more Americans now who are drinking fine wines, and they like to try something new on a night out. If you do not yet have a good knowledge of wine, make the next book you read one on that subject. Soon you'll know *Vitis vinifera* from *Vitis labrusca,* dry from sweet, and varietals from all over. The stocking of wines is discussed in chapter 7.

Why should a server get upset by an occasional small tip when he or she has given good service? The same service to another customer will elicit a very large tip on a different occasion. As with other things in life, it all averages out.

Taking the Order

There are several ways to handle taking orders. Most restaurants today use either a single guest check or one that is prepared in duplicate. If you keep your alcoholic beverage records separate, you may, in addition, use a separate bar check. The advantage of a two-part guest check is that while the chef works from one copy, the server can refer to the other for preparing drinks, serving the correct salad dressing, and recalling special instructions. If a single check is used, the server must either remember everything well or constantly refer to the order wheel. Of course, in the good old days, everyone was expected to remember everything and nothing was written down. That kind of server and chef is an endangered species, but they provide a goal to strive for. Don't ever let anyone tell you that being a waitress or a waiter is for dummies. To be an excellent one requires the highest intelligence and sensitivity.

One of the nicest phrases on a menu is this: "Whenever possible, we will be happy to accommodate your special tastes or dietary needs." The management can decide whether "whenever possible" is now, but it is usually easy to accommodate people who cannot eat this or that.

Special Orders

Do not permit your customers to reserve one of your special menu items for the time they plan to arrive. If you run out of the special before they get there, you run out. There is nothing more annoying to your other customers than to be told that the special is gone, only to see it served half an hour later to people who were seated after them. This does not apply to special non-menu items that have been prearranged between the patron and the chef.

Serving the Wine

There is no great mystery to traditional wine service at the table. If you are serving a good selection of American wines, the quality of one year's vintage may not vary much from another year's. Nevertheless, the traditional tasting ritual still has an important purpose: to determine whether the particular bottle being served has kept well. If a dry or faulty cork has allowed air to oxidize (maderize) the wine, or to cause it to turn sour, these faults will be discernible by sight and smell, as well as by taste. The tasting ritual is designed to avoid serving the customer a bad bottle of wine. The routine is simple and logical:

- Deliver the wine to the table as soon as possible after it is ordered.

- The opening and tasting should take place before food is served so the diner has a clear palate. If possible, the diner should be asked whether he or she prefers to have the bottle of a "bigger" red wine opened and given time to "breathe" before it is drunk.

- White and rosé wines should be served slightly chilled, but not so cold that the fruity bouquet is dulled.

- Red wine should be served at room temperature, which means about 60°F (room temperature before central heating was invented).

- Always show the label to allow the customer to verify the wine selection and vintage, if any. I recommend that the server quietly mention the basic data, saying something such as, "Full bottle of Pedroncelli Pinot Noir, 2001, for you, madam."

- Red wine, especially older bottles, should not be jostled, so that any sediment remains at the bottom of the bottle.

- The foil cover must be cut well below the lip of the bottle to ensure that no taste of whatever may have developed under it is imparted to the wine. The occasional residue and mold uncovered at the top of the cork and bottle lip should be carefully wiped away. The use of various plastic covers with perforations already built in allows easy removal.

- The wine glasses should be of clear glass, with a capacity of about 8 to 10 ounces.

- Smelling the cork is the first way to detect any potential problem. It should smell of wine, not corky or musty. The server should remove the cork from the corkscrew and hand it to the person who ordered the wine.

- A small amount of wine is poured into the glass of the person who ordered it. Tip the top of the bottle close to the glass and finish the maneuver by gently resting the neck of the bottle on the edge of the glass and twisting the bottle a quarter turn as the tip is lifted. This will halt the flow without having any wine run down the neck of the bottle.

- Wait patiently while the wine is swirled around the glass to release more wine molecules into the air in the glass, which is then held up to the nose so the bouquet can be noted. The color and clarity of the wine will also be examined against a source of light.

- When the wine is tasted and found to be sound, pour not more than half a glassful for each of the rest of the party, usually starting with the women at the table, before returning to finish filling the glass of the taster.

- Place the bottle on the table where the host of the party can easily reach it. For chilled wines, if you provide an insulated bucket to keep the remainder ready to serve, be sure to leave a small towel or napkin draped over the bucket to use for wiping away moisture from the bottom of the bottle, especially if the patron will be refilling glasses. Better yet, the server or maitre d' should keep a close watch on the table and appear at the right time to do the job. Most wine drinkers will appreciate the attention, but they can let you know if they prefer to handle it themselves. Close attention to a larger party will also allow you to bring an additional bottle, if desired, at the most appropriate time during the meal.

House or bar wine, served from an open bottle or decanter, is not subject to the tasting ritual, for obvious reasons.

The service of champagne (or sparkling wine) can be dangerous if not undertaken with caution. Champagne should be more chilled than white still wine, to about 40°F. The bottle should be carefully brought to the table in an ice bucket large enough to keep the whole bottle chilled through a leisurely dinner. After verification of the label, return the bottle to the bucket and remove the wire or other hood by placing the thumb of one hand over the top of the cork; the string hood is cut or the wire loop is held firmly with the other hand while it is worked up and down rapidly until the wire breaks. The cork may then be removed by grasping it firmly between the thumb and forefinger and rocking it back and forth as it is pulled carefully out while holding the bottle at a slight angle. The carbonation pressure of the champagne will sometimes shoot the cork out at a very high speed—sufficient to cause an eye injury or break an overhead light fixture. Therefore, an inexperienced server should first drape a clean napkin over the top of the bottle, then remove the wire hood and cork under its protection. If the bottle is properly chilled and has not been jostled, the champagne should not bubble out. If the cork is held very close to the top of the bottle upon removal, it can sometimes prevent spilling while allowing enough gas to escape to relieve the pressure.

Enforcing Alcoholic Beverage Control Laws

For a restaurant serving fermented spirits but no hard liquor, the requirement to prevent underage persons from imbibing can be an annoying one to comply with. In most states, the failure to do so can cost both the server and the licensee a lot of money. Check with your local authorities to see how they expect you to do it, so that in the case where you are fooled by a forged I.D. you will be off the hook.

"How Is Everything?"

Within a few minutes after delivery of the main course, the server should return to the table to ask this question. Even if there are no complaints, this creates the feeling that the management cares about whether the food is being enjoyed. It also provides an opportunity for the server to check on the need for more water, butter, bread, or wine. The diners also have the chance to ask for anything extra they may have neglected to order.

Desserts

The difference between just having a reputation for good food and getting rave reviews may hinge on whether or not you offer special desserts. Homemade desserts are the denouement, the major scene of Act III. If your dessert offerings don't vary much from day to day, it may be best to put them on the menu. However, the way your servers describe the desserts can mean the difference between a customer ordering one or passing up the final course.

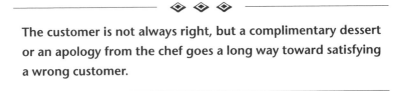

The customer is not always right, but a complimentary dessert or an apology from the chef goes a long way toward satisfying a wrong customer.

You may prefer to include dessert in the dinner price, but that is not really fair to those who never eat desserts. The dessert portions need not be large; they are worth a fair price even for a small after-dinner size.

You may find people ordering a dessert item they have enjoyed at lunch, if you also serve that meal. Remember, on a busy dinner shift few servers are eager to make hot-fudge sundaes for a party of eight.

If you become well known for your excellent homemade desserts, you cannot afford to serve *only* dessert at night to any party, assuming yours is a small place with few tables. Once you make the rule, don't break it, even for friends.

Handling an Error

Restaurant patrons who are somehow displeased by the food rather than by the service itself commonly conclude that they should leave a meager tip or even none. But the size of the tip should not be reduced unless they have received poor or indifferent service; diners should not vent on the server their displeasure with the kitchen. In most cases of error or dissatisfaction, the server and the management are eager to rectify it, if they are notified in time to do so. This is the reason the server or maitre d' stops at the table to ask if everything is satisfactory. That is the time for anything amiss to be reported and set right. Depending on the chef's and the management's policy, items returned to the kitchen for further cooking or because of dissatisfaction with the preparation, tenderness, or taste are usually handled on an individual basis.

The biggest favor you can do for a small restaurant owner is to recommend the place to a friend. The next biggest is to give him your honest, calm opinion about your experience at his restaurant. If you are pleased, everyone feels rewarded for their efforts. If you are dissatisfied, the owner can try to eliminate the problem.

It is generally only the most experienced and relaxed diners who have the self-confidence to report something gone wrong, especially if only one dinner out of four at the table is not right. But a sharp server can usually spot the sidelong glance between two diners, the turned-down corners of someone's mouth, and the mumbled response, "It's okay, never mind, Mildred," as sure signs of repressed distress. A gentle "Are you sure? We would like you to enjoy everything," may elicit the actual complaint. Sometimes it is simple. "My husband *hates* broccoli." Or, "This steak is really a little tough." If the management cares, something can be substituted for broccoli and perhaps another choice of entrée can be allowed for the tough steak. At least a complimentary dessert or glass of wine may make everyone feel better.

Whenever you have to deal with an unhappy customer, think about how you can convert him from a disgruntled person who may tell all his friends how much he disliked your place into one who will tell them how well you treated him despite the problem.

One evening, a regular customer at our restaurant responded to my question about his dinner with, "The lamb is a little chewy." And I believed him when he said it tasted good and he would not like another dinner choice. But after he had paid the check and departed with his wife, I had occasion to have a slice of lamb roast for my own dinner. A little chewy, indeed! It was, for some inexplicable reason, as rubbery as an inner tube, though it did taste good. The chef had cut it with a very sharp slicing knife and had not discovered its condition. Luckily, I knew my customer's number, and I immediately phoned him to apologize. He laughed, but graciously accepted a rain check for another lamb dinner on the house, which he collected with pleasure a few weeks later. You may think it was costly to respond that way when the patron was willing to accept a little toughness in the meat. But this couple told everyone in town about how they had been treated. The good feelings engendered by such concern were worth far more to our reputation than the cost of the second dinner.

Of course, the crass customer may take advantage of you. One evening when a couple complained of a tough steak *after* they had eaten all of it, their unhappiness was so believable that we subtracted the cost of the meat from the dinner price, just to be nice. After they had paid the reduced bill and left smiling, the people at the adjacent table, somewhat vexed at what they had witnessed, confided to the waitress that I had been "taken in." They said the couple had shared the steak and eaten it with gusto, exclaiming how delicious it was. So you must set a dining room policy that allows the chef to verify all complaints of toughness, lack of fresh taste or smell, or other problems.

Busing

Busing of tables is one of the dining room procedures that reveals the basic character of a restaurant. The demand for fast clearing and resetting of tables will be highest at your peak business hours. If you do not employ buspersons, the servers will be hard-pressed to do the job.

Teamwork is the key to proper busing. If each server is expected to bus the tables he serves, the routine will be less smooth than if all servers try to bus and reset any tables that become vacant. The servers must understand that making a table available for the next party is just as important as any other part of the job. The only tasks that have higher priority are delivering hot food or taking care of a spill. The entire serving and busing routine is made simpler if the servers follow one basic rule: Never leave the dining room empty-handed. If something is carried back to the dish room on each ordinary trip, the tables will be kept relatively clear as they become available for resetting.

For busing to be done with proper form, a tray must be used to clear the dirty dishes and silverware. It should be a strict rule that glasses and cups are not to be picked up or carried by inserting the fingers into the tops. This rule is not based solely on form; it has health implications as well. Organisms from the lips of the previous customer could be transferred by the server's fingers to the next plate of food served, thence to the diner. Although this is highly unlikely, it is possible. Besides, it looks tacky. The use of a tray allows just as many glasses to be carried with style.

Noisy table clearing is both inelegant and annoying to the entire dining room. It is no more necessary to make noise when clearing a table than it is when serving it. Usually, it is the silverware that makes the most noise. If the utensils are carefully gathered and handled firmly, rather than left sprawled across the plates, they will make much less clatter. The main advantage to the padded dining table and tablecloth is noise reduction.

It takes extra time to replace a dirty tablecloth, but a clean cloth is more important than a little extra time. Some restaurants compromise by using a wipeable mat or cross drape on the table to cushion the plate and silverware. A paper placemat serves the same purpose, but the waste and loss of class it represents seem not worth the trouble, at least for dinner service. The only advantage to the paper placemat is that it is possible to print your menu on it; it might be a good way to handle breakfast or lunch.

When the scene is reset at the table for the next diner, the props should all be in place. As stage manager, the maitre d' should check the setting before raising the curtain. The bottom edges of each of the pieces of silverware should be set along an imaginary line parallel to the edge of the table. Whatever is in the center of the table—salt, pepper, and sweetener packet holders at the minimum—should be wiped clean of fingerprints and neatly arranged. If there are fresh flowers on the table, as there are in most excellent restaurants, there should be no wilted ones left in the arrangement. And the "reserved seat" is worse than "standing-room only" in the waiting room if that seat contains any food or beverage residue from the last performance. There are few moments more mortifying for the maitre d' than when he pulls back the chair for a lovely lady in dinner dress and discovers the lasagna sauce on the seat just as she lowers herself into it.

Food service and table busing are roles in a ballet. Coordination and smooth, quiet movements are essential. This does not mean there is no place for exuberance, humor, and natural responses to troublesome or funny situations. But loud directions or wise-guy responses must not originate with your staff. One of the unmistakable signs of a good dining room staff is that when a patron makes a request of someone other than the server assigned to his table, the request is fulfilled immediately. This kind of cooperation is also reflected in the speed and finesse with which two people clear and set a table for the next party.

Dining Room "No-Noes"

There are a few "no-noes" in a dining room. Absolutely no visible or audible anger from the staff is to be permitted in a dining room with customers in it. No loud drunks or abusive customers who are disturbing your other guests should be allowed to remain in the restaurant. The same is true for a screeching child, although occasionally the youngster can be placated with an offer of finger food, such as sliced fruit, bread sticks, raisins, or crackers; try chipped ice for the sore gums of a teething infant.

You may wish to discourage infants altogether in your place, especially if the room is really small. The interests and comfort of the majority of your guests take precedence over the inconvenience to the parents—who should not have brought a tired, irritable child into your restaurant in the first place. You may have to suggest quietly, gently, but firmly that the child be taken out of the dining room. If there are two parents present, they can take turns caring for the infant and still get a meal eaten. If you can do so, encourage the parents by offering to keep food warm for the unlucky adult who is walking outside with the baby. You can offer to provide the rest of the meal in take-home containers without suffering continued dining room disturbance. You run the risk of losing a customer, but there are a few people who are so insensitive to others in a restaurant that you are probably better off without their business anyway.

Customer Out of Control

If you serve liquor or if a customer arrives at your restaurant under the influence of alcohol, there is a chance that the drinker will get out of control. Yours is the position of authority, so do not hesitate to use it. Your other customers will appreciate and respect you for it. But proceed with caution. Your servers should be the first to alert you to a potential problem. The person serving the table should exert polite but firm pressure on the unruly customer by telling him to lower his voice and cease the disturbance, or else he will have to leave.

If you are not happy with the results, you should reinforce the message personally in a calm, steady voice, without a smile. If there seems to be someone else at the table who is more rational, or who seems upset by the boorish behavior, a quiet appeal for his assistance may help. It is fair to state that you have received a complaint about the behavior of the offender(s) at that table. (You have. The server notified you.)

> When a customer becomes more and more demanding, impatient, and unreasonable, it is necessary for the server to become correspondingly more calm, responsive, and sweet—up to a point. When the tolerance threshold has been passed, it is time for the host or senior server to take over the table, so that other customers are not affected by the breach.

Often, an intoxicated party intent on making trouble will make loud complaints about the food or service or both. Your strongest urge may be to try to get them out of your place as quickly as possible, and in fact that may be the best course of action. However, you should consider this: If they entered your place heavily under the influence, and especially if you served them even one glass of wine, it is best for you and the public that they finish a meal and have some black coffee. If they drive off and later cause injury to anyone, including themselves or a passenger, their victim has legal recourse against you if you served the driver any alcohol. Do not hesitate, therefore, to tell an intoxicated patron that you are concerned about his ability to drive and insist that he have a complimentary cup of coffee.

Under no circumstances should you tolerate any verbal or physical abuse of anyone. For example, if an unruly customer touches a server in a way that is degrading, you should take definitive action to put a stop to it. This applies to sober as well as drunk customers.

I need not list all the circumstances that might cause you to call upon law enforcement assistance; the laws and your rights and obligations as an owner of a public restaurant are different in each state. Before you need them, you should find occasion to discuss this subject with your local police. Find out how long it will take after a phone call to have a patrol car at your front door. Discuss how best to handle a customer who is disturbing your dining room, destroying property, assaulting or battering someone, or trying to avoid paying the bill. Follow their advice. Never use unnecessary force. You have a lot to lose if you permanently injure even a misbehaving customer. These cases are so rare in a nice small restaurant that you will probably never have to deal with them. But be prepared.

Presenting the Check

In the best of the old-time restaurants, the check was never presented until it was asked for. In your small place, you may not be able to wait that long, and you should find a way for the server or maitre d' to ask whether the check may be presented. On especially busy nights, you will probably want to do it as soon as possible after it is determined that everything the party might desire has been offered.

In many parts of the country these days, younger restaurant employees are using the vernacular phrase "you guys" when addressing customers. They many not even realize they are saying it, but it is your fault if they continue. In every instance, the word "you" suffices, as in, "How are you," or "What can I get for you," rather than ". . . you guys." Train your staff.

The check should be delivered on a plate or tip tray. Often this is a very good time for the maitre d' to ask how the entire meal was enjoyed. Sometimes customers are confused about who will take their money—the server, the maitre d', or a cashier at the front desk. A word of explanation will help. Also, mentioning the forms of payment that are acceptable—such as credit cards, personal checks, traveler's checks, or cash—will help them decide.

If you accept credit cards using a manual system, be sure to imprint the card data legibly. The modern card authorization systems use automatic printing. Carefully note the name on the card when you return to the table for the signature on the draft. Nowadays, the card may well belong to a woman in the party, who may become annoyed if you place the draft for signature in front of her male companion.

One of the saddest events in a fine restaurant occurs when two grown people begin to argue over who will pay the check. I have seen people enter in a fine, happy mood, only to leave in a pout because of a silly argument over the check. Wise people either compromise or acquiesce graciously when confronted. But you can assist in this matter by establishing a hard and fast rule: "Whoever asks for the check first, gets it." That usually will put an end to the argument for a while.

When you go out to dinner and you are particularly pleased by your meal (and if you can afford it), send a tip in to the chef.

For some parties, especially a large one or one in which both male and female guests are being entertained by a female host, you will occasionally be asked not to present the check at the table. In this case, some convenient arrangement can be made, using a credit card or personal check perhaps, to pay the check afterward. If the check is normally delivered to the table by the server, you will want to be certain to remind him of the special arrangement sometime before the end of the meal.

Retrieving the Table

One of the restaurateur's more tactful arts is getting a party that has finished dinner and paid the check to relinquish the table. Normally, this can be accomplished by asking whether more coffee is desired or whether anything else can be brought. There are also various body language signals, ESP transmissions, scowls, glares, and grimaces—all designed to convey a succinct message without actually asking for the table at the risk of antagonizing a satisfied customer. The technique exists in its highest form in a small restaurant, where there are few tables and demand for them is high. When there are people with reservations waiting, and a previous party seems to think they have rented their table for the evening, each minute that the agonized host must endure takes five minutes off his life.

Do your favorite small restaurant owner a favor. If you plan to linger over dinner, either invite him sincerely to tell you when he needs the table for another party or make reservations for a later time so you are the last occupants of your table for the night. When the music is turned off, the lights are turned up, and the vacuum cleaner appears at the next table, you will know it is time to go home.

Follow the Script

I believe that the use of slang by a restaurant's staff can be a contributing factor to sloppiness in service. Informality and homeyness can be achieved without careless speech. Train all the "players" in your restaurant to deliver their lines professionally, usually with a smile. They sound like this:

- "Good evening. How many in your party?"

- "Your table is ready, Mr. Priapadophalus; please follow me."

- "Our specials tonight are poached trout or fresh coho salmon, with herb butter and lemon wine sauce. Sheree will be right with you to take your order."

- "Hello, Mr. Priapadophalus; nice to see you tonight. I'll be right with you. Have you seen the wine list? We have a great new Pinot Grigio."

- "Are you ready to order? Please take your time. I'll send Daniel over to discuss the wine list. And then I'll be right back to take your order."

- "Do you prefer dry or less dry wine? Well, then I suggest a very special Alsatian style by one of our local wineries. It is the dry Gewürtztraminer by Claiborne and Churchill. I'm sorry, we have that only in the full bottle. I'll bring it right away."

- "This wine is 2004 vintage and you'll note that it is estate bottled. That means that the grapes from which this wine was made were grown in their own vineyards. Will you taste, sir? Thank you. Enjoy your dinners."

- "May I take your order? How would you like your steak prepared, sir? Our house dressing is an herb-vinegar-and-oil, or you may have blue cheese, honey-mustard, or pepper-parmesan. Would you like sour cream or butter with your baked potato? Tonight's fresh vegetable is steamed cauliflower with fresh hollandaise sauce. Yes, I'll bring the sauce on the side. May I bring your soup now, or would you prefer to sip your wine for a few minutes? Thank you."

- "Our special soup tonight is a homemade vegetable with leeks, available in a cup or bowl."

- "Have you finished? May I remove your plate? Thank you. Yes, the server will bring hot sourdough rolls with your salad in just a moment."

- "Would you like some fresh-ground black pepper on your salad?"

- "Would you like to keep your salad? Your entrée will be served in just a moment."

- "Broiled salmon for you, madam, and poached trout for you, sir."

- "Are your dinners all right here, gentlemen?"

- "Would you like to have one of our homemade desserts tonight?"

- "We have a variety of teas available. Would you like lemon with your tea?"

- "Is there anything else I may bring for you?"

- "I'm glad you enjoyed your dinners tonight. May I bring your check?"

- "I'll take your card and be right back with the receipt for your signature."

- "Don't forget to take your card and your copy of the receipt. It was a pleasure to serve you. Thank you."

Find occasion to listen to the way each server describes your menu items and the methods of preparation. A good server will find a choice of words that enhances the description by making it sound as appetizing as possible. If an item is baked or broiled, it should be described as coming out "moist" or "juicy"—if it is in fact served that way. It is better to say "juicy" than "not dry," and "sautéed in butter" rather than "pan-fried." Say "prepared to your order" rather than "cooked here." It is better to say "a delicious blend of . . ." rather than "a mixture of . . .," and so on. Remember, it's an evening of theater.

7

Getting Supplied

S TAPLES, FRESH PRODUCE, fresh seafood, aged beef, lean lamb, meaty bacon, fresh pork sausage, pastry flour, olive oil, fresh lox, fine wines . . . where does all that stuff come from? Where, indeed. Who you get your supplies from can mean the difference between serving a high-quality meal and something better off forgotten.

Suppliers and Services

Here is a partial list of products and services you may require:

1. Groceries and staples

2. Meat and poultry

3. Seafood

4. Produce

5. Milk, cheese, and other dairy products

6. Bread and bakery items

7. Special ethnic food staples

8. Coffee and tea

9. Wine and beer

10. Soft drinks and juices

11. Linen supply and laundering

12. Dishwashing machine supply and service

13. Water softener service

14. Cleaning and maintenance products

15. Gardening service

16. Printed material or computer/printer supplies and service

Many of these items can be supplied by the same vendor. For example, fine cheeses may come from the dairy supplier, the meat and poultry supplier, or a special vendor. Your wine list may be printed by your wine distributor. There are several miscellaneous services you may require that are not listed. These include knife sharpening, steam cleaning, carpet cleaning, window washing, sign painting, and trash and edible garbage pickup. In addition, you will require a convenient source for small equipment and utensil replacement. If there is a local restaurant supply store, it will serve. Otherwise, your groceries and staples supplier will probably have a catalog from which you can choose such items, with full return and refund privileges.

Selecting Suppliers

It is likely you will open in an area that already has at least one reasonably good restaurant. Check with the management there to find out which suppliers serve the area. But also consider the possibility that a better supplier may be willing to expand its operation to serve a new restaurant, even if it is not now delivering in the area.

If you are in a locale new to you, try to get an interview with a retired chef in the vicinity who cooked for or ran a successful restaurant. Find out which products and companies he or she held in high regard. If that is not possible, go to a nearby town or city; the chef in the best restaurant there may be willing to discuss suppliers. Call her up and talk over your plans and menu with her. The ultimate choice of who gets the bulk of your orders rests with you. You have no obligations to any particular supplier. It is a good idea to try to have at least two suppliers for all major items in your food inventory. It keeps everyone on his or her toes and often helps you take advantage of the bargains that only the salesperson can bring to your attention each week.

Your choice of which day of the week to remain closed, if you have that option, may hinge on which day certain important suppliers' salespeople stop at your place. You should be open for them, if possible. If you are closed that day, you may have to be at the restaurant anyway for the first few months to see the sales representative and get to know the line. You can very likely place your orders via e-mail or by telephone. There is never a "best" day to close—only best days to be open.

Pickup or Delivery?

Most suppliers of staple goods—such as grocery items, paper and cleaning products, and other packaged goods—make deliveries once a week. Fresh food suppliers will appear at least twice a week with such items as fruits and vegetables, meat, seafood, and dairy products. In the city, you may be able to get daily delivery, if necessary. With once-a-week delivery, your salesperson becomes a key link in the chain that saves you when you have forgotten to order something or the supplier has forgotten to load it on the truck. If he cares about you, he may be able to make a special trip to get it to you or send it up the next day with another supplier's truck coming your way.

In some remote areas, you may not find competing suppliers to serve you well. Under such circumstances, you may be forced to arrange with someone in a nearby town or city that is served by a good supplier to accept deliveries, which will be picked up later by you or your helper. Such arrangements are very inconvenient and expensive at best; perhaps in a mountain resort or other remote tourist area the effort is justifiable. There is simply no substitute for reliable, high-quality supplies delivered to your door.

In general, it is worth more to you to have something delivered than to go somewhere to pick it up. You will always be offered cash-and-carry bargains in provisions at restaurant supply warehouses. But if you figure your time at $15 per hour, you usually come out the loser.

Is It Really the Best Buy?

When you use canned staples in your kitchen, take care to compare price per *net weight* pound, as well as the taste. Comparison of the case prices alone of two suppliers will not give the cost of the food accurately unless the yield per can is the same. For example, a quart can of tomatoes from one company may contain 20 percent more water than that of another company. The latter may be priced 5 percent higher, but it is actually the better buy in most instances. The salesperson of the higher-priced tomatoes will be happy to make an actual drain-and-weigh comparison test right in your kitchen. The old adage is generally still true: You get what you pay for. It's your job not to pay for water at the price of tomatoes.

The Salesperson Is the Key

No supplier is perfect, nor is any salesperson. But the difference between one good supplier and another is the sales representative. He or she is your link to the company, whose office and warehouse may be in another city. How well you evaluate and choose your sales reps will make the difference between good and unreliable service.

Several weeks before you open your restaurant, you will be besieged by all sorts of salespeople trying to sell you frozen food, unnecessary items of small equipment, and their special brands of goods. They will be testing you to see what you know, trying to get you started on their particular lines of products; they know that once you are hooked, you may be too busy or reluctant to change. Some may try to intimidate you into taking a minimum $500 order before they will agree to sell you the very thing that you called them about specifically. Never be intimidated by a sales rep. Here again, your ability to judge character is essential to the selection process.

The best sales representatives see their role as problem solvers, not just salespeople. Some of them have been in your shoes in a previous life, when they owned or ran a food service operation. Do not be put off by a probing question about how a particular selection on your menu is selling. If you have already learned that your sales rep has the experience and understands your goals, you may benefit from an astute observation or suggestion on trying something new or different. The best of such reps will always find a way to solve an unexpected shortage or misdelivery by having another of his nearby customers, such as a meat market, make a loan of your desperately needed item. You must always keep the salesperson's cell phone number handy, as well as his or her home phone number.

A favorite trick of slightly slippery salespeople is to quote an attractive price for an expensive item, such as canned white albacore tuna; upon delivery, you discover that an unfamiliar brand has been substituted for your tried-and-true regular brand. Or the invoice price on delivery may be higher than the one quoted when you placed the order. Obviously, you must check each order when it arrives. Unintentional errors will occur occasionally, but the scrupulous sales rep will take pains to correct them. The case of substitute goods will be picked up with no argument, and you will receive credit for it or the invoice price will be reduced to the figure at which you ordered the goods. The latter case will be unlikely if the sales rep is deliberately "low-balling." If it happens too often, it may be time to call the district manager or find a new supplier.

Eventually, someone will inadvertently fill the chef's sugar canister with salt. If this is the worst mix-up in your restaurant, you will be fortunate. But it reminds you how important it is to taste what you serve. Moreover, it shows how imperative it is never to store any nonfood substance, such as cleaning powder, insecticide, deicing compound, or other potentially dangerous items, in a place or container where it could be mistaken for a look-alike food ingredient.

The effective way to buy foods for your restaurant is to interview as many suppliers as are available in the region, or at least four or five if there is an abundance of them. Tell each that you will require the selected vendors to provide you with a weekly price/inventory guide via fax, e-mail, or hand delivery on Sunday or Monday morning, with prices valid for that entire week. Explain to each that you will be selecting your supplier based not only on price but also on other factors, such as brands, specialty items, customer service, and accuracy of delivery and billing. Also advise them that you will keep track of their performance and their company might achieve the status as your "primary vendor," which means that they will get the bulk of your order even if another supplier offers an item for 50 cents less on a particular week. Then decide on two of the candidates for your business and use them to compete for your favor. The crucial factor in implementing a primary vendor strategy is to make clear that you compare the market prices weekly and factor in performance measures, such as how often delivery shortages occur and how they are handled. The range of prices the sales reps can quote you allows them to work with you to achieve profits for all. Your volume of business, of course, is a key factor.

The nationwide network of rapid delivery service that has spread in the past two decades to cover all the urban and many of the less densely populated regions may help you be successful. If your clientele and price structure can support it, you may not be limited to local suppliers for everything. Can you prepare a favorite food from some other region of the country that you can successfully introduce to your customers as a special once a month? With overnight or two-day delivery, appropriately packed fresh or frozen items can be yours via such service. Live lobsters from Maine come to mind immediately, but the possibilities are endless. Special herbs, vegetables, or fruits may be the talk of the town if you do something unusual or nontraditional with them. Finding suppliers in other regions of the country is now just a matter of doing an Internet search with the right key words. Once you find one, you may be led to others in your own area by word of mouth. This is especially true among organic produce suppliers who know each other and cooperate.

Inventory Control

Inventory control for a small restaurant can be done quite simply if the storage shelves allow you to display your staples so that all items in stock are visually obvious. Weekly ordering thus becomes a matter of simply taking note of the stock on hand as you walk around with your order sheet. You can supplement your visual check by keeping a "needs list" for unusual or infrequently ordered items. Many suppliers will provide you with a printed order sheet on which you can mark each week's order. If you have Internet access from your computer, you may be able to log on to a supplier's Web site and enter your order electronically in the middle of the night or very early in the morning. If so, make sure you know the cutoff time for orders for a scheduled delivery day. If your salesperson is savvy, he may warn you of an impending price increase in time for you to stock up on continually needed items; it is usually impractical, though, to hoard too much of any one thing.

Adequate storage and refrigeration capacity will enable you to take advantage of occasional special price cuts and should increase your profit. But the ability to hold down waste is even more important to steady profits. That will depend on your imagination in using leftovers and on your keeping accurate records to help you plan from year to year.

Delivery Routine

Many sales and delivery people will walk through your back door and into your kitchen every week. Some will be regulars, who will soon learn your routine and will place the delivery where you expect to find it, or will try to avoid making a sales call right in the middle of a busy lunch. But occasionally there will be temporary replacements—a deliveryperson who needs a kind word about where everything goes or who arrives when you have no time and stands right in the middle of the kitchen. Relax. He can wait a few minutes while you finish, or you can get someone else to check the order and initial the invoice.

There is a lot to be said for making your kitchen environment one that the delivery people look forward to visiting. If the chef is glad to see the deliverer, and perhaps asks some friendly personal question, it helps make a boring day more pleasant. Occasionally, a nice cool drink (no alcohol, please!) or even a short lunch can be offered. Too often the delivery person becomes the recipient of each restaurant owner's petty grievance of the day. And if these small kindnesses are not in themselves reward enough, think of this: Sales and delivery people see and talk to many, many people in their travels. Their friends and acquaintances expect them to know the good places to eat; when they speak highly of you and your restaurant, the benefit is limitless.

Dishwashing Machine Service

Of all the suppliers whose efforts do not involve food or beverage, the dishwashing supply person is the most important. When you unexpectedly run out of soap, he must respond promptly. Do not deal with anyone who will not also be able to service and repair your brand of equipment. That should mean that he carries with him a good inventory of parts, or can get them at a moment's notice. In this instance, again, the price of the soap and rinse additive may be lower elsewhere, but the availability of regular service and repairs is worth much more.

One never knows when your service people will find a chance to help you beyond the call of duty. One afternoon when it was supposed to be a normally quiet off-season day in our town, the unexpected occurred. A very large tour bus pulled up to our restaurant and disgorged its contents of hungry tourists, while a frantic tour guide asked if we could handle them. Our staff at that moment consisted of three people—a chef, a waitress, and myself—and there were 10 indoor tables and 11 outdoor tables, most of which filled rapidly. I am not a chef, nor am I a really convincing waitress, but I do wield a mean wipe cloth as a busperson and I'm pretty fast with a credit-card imprinter as a cashier. My professional dishwashing experience dates from 1950, but under circumstances like this, everyone becomes the dishwasher as often as possible. It was too late to call for help, even if any had been available.

If you serve tourists, you and your staff may someday be unnerved by the following occurrence. One perfectly ordinary day, a big gray tour bus from Indiana will stop and a nice man will enter your establishment. You will be told tremulously that 44 hungry people are coming in, ready or not. Their impatience to eat will be exceeded only by their inability to decide what they want. When the first one is served, half of the other guests will rise to see what she got, and 50 percent of them will try to change their orders. They will drive your servers to distraction with a series of ill-timed requests, culminating with the demand for separate checks. They will all pay with $20 bills. They will each leave $1 under the edge of a plate, although they loved your food and service. The above symptoms of acute constipation are a common tour-bus syndrome. The cure is to get home.

In the middle of this madhouse, when we were running out of cups, forks, iced-tea glasses, and who knows what else, who should arrive but the dishwashing machine serviceman. I spotted him on one wild pass through the kitchen and saw him smile as I shouted, "No time now!" For the next hour, on each of my trips into the kitchen with bus trays full of dirty dishes, I saw that he was still there—not working on the machine, but doing the dishes. He saved the day, the tour, and the frazzled nerves of the staff. He got more than a free lunch. He got our continued patronage when he left his company and went into the distributing and service business for himself. We could have gone with another reliable, larger firm whose product was cheaper, but one does not quickly forget service beyond what is expected.

Fresh or Frozen?

The pressures on restaurateurs to use other than locally grown or produced foods are very great. The vagaries of both season and suppliers tend to force you to rely on your can opener and your freezer, rather than on your local farmer, fisherman, or herdsman. The following comments are intended as counterpressure.

Seafood

Timeliness is a key to reliability, whether in a supplier or an employee. But if you specialize in serving truly fresh seafood, you will be subject to the unpredictability of the ocean, the weather, the fishing fleet, and the people who fillet fish. You will have to learn to trade off the uncertainty of delivery against the desire to serve fish that is delivered the day you serve it. (Not that it is so bad to serve fish delivered yesterday, but if you have some left over, you will gain an extra day of use if it is fresh the first day.) You will learn to recognize by touch and smell whether your fish is truly fresh upon delivery. Do not tolerate any old fish. Freshness in seafood is more important than whether it arrives exactly when promised. One advantage of having a small restaurant is that, in an emergency when an order fails to arrive, you can usually get enough of any item at a local market to get you through the day.

Some types of seafood are best delivered frozen to ensure freshness, unless you are absolutely certain of the local source of supply. These include individually quick-frozen (IQF) shrimp and prawns of all sizes, chopped clams, scallops, squid, abalone, lobster tails, king crab legs, and Midwestern trout. (Note: The size of prawns, or shrimp, is designated "under x," where x equals the number of prawns it takes to make a pound; so with "under 12s," each prawn is $1\frac{1}{3}$ ounces or more in size.) Shellfish and crustaceans spoil rapidly once they are dead. The likelihood of freshness is greater when they are packaged frozen for shipment. Clams, oysters, and mussels are best served fresh. Frozen clams in the shell are available but not recommended.

I strongly urge you, however, to establish the reputation that when your menu says "fresh," it means the seafood served has never been frozen. It shows.

Produce

Fresh produce is essential to a menu that attempts to offer a well-balanced, nutritionally excellent meal. As the public becomes more aware of nutritional value, you will be able to establish a reputation for providing a healthful experience, as well as an elegant and joyful one. After all, isn't that what is meant by a "home-cooked" meal: one that is well planned, nutritionally balanced, and served promptly after preparation? It is not difficult to serve fresh vegetables that have not been overcooked, and the seasonal changes in the fresh produce market build variety into your menu.

You will be able to find someone who will deliver fresh produce if you will be a steady customer. It is cheaper to order by the full or half crate or carton. The growing number of people who have cut down their intake of meat have made it profitable to prepare vegetarian lunch and dinner offerings. Identify menu items created from fresh vegetables and fruits that are in demand as a main course or as an appetizer. If the latter, some patrons will order one as their main item with soup or salad, wine, and a nice dessert, to create a special dinner. Your reputation for fresh fruit and vegetables will grow, and you will create the demand that will allow you to order in more economical bulk quantities.

Especially during the summer, you will get offers from itinerant produce vendors who specialize in tomatoes, lettuce, avocados, sweet corn, or the like. They will offer to supply you with all your produce, with big savings on their specialty. This is great while it lasts, but the reliability of a fresh food source over the entire year is worth a lot to you. Don't be too quick to switch from your old dependable supplier on price differential alone.

All produce vendors will give you the choicest goods when you first become a customer. It won't last. But if the produce delivered is partly rotten, or too old to last until the next delivery, be very firm about receiving credit. This should not happen too often. If it does, it may be time for a competitor to have a chance.

Beef

Beef is not what it was when feed corn was cheaper. To ensure proper flavor and tenderness, it will be necessary to age your beef an additional amount of time. This means that the sealed polyethylene bag in which, for example, a top sirloin is delivered *must* be intact, and it must remain so during cold storage. If there is blood in the bottom of a carton of "tops," it means that one of the sealed bags is punctured, and you don't want that piece of meat unless you plan to use it immediately. Send back punctured packages if you plan to age the contents.

On occasion, there may be other reasons for returning meat. Discuss in advance with your sales representative the return policy for his or her company, and make clear what you will not accept. For example, you should return items of the wrong cut, the wrong weight (significantly different from what you ordered), or the wrong portion size (chops cut at three to the pound, say, instead of four to the pound), or meat that is improperly trimmed so that there is much too much fat. If a customer reports a really tough steak (not ordered well done) and you have just cut it from a new piece, you may wish to be able to return the unused portion; this should be arranged in advance with the salesperson. (Perhaps you will be grinding your own beef and can make some use of the tough meat anyway, but that would be pretty expensive ground beef.)

The main point is that you must train your meat supplier to provide you with the very best quality or the item will be returned. If you are small enough to use selected meat cuts, yet big enough to be a steady customer, you should be able to insist on the best. Again, the reliability of a supplier who sends you top-quality meat is worth the few cents more per pound you may have to pay.

Truth in Menu Descriptions

Tell the truth on your menu. If the food is fresh, say so. If it is "fresh frozen," and the customer asks the server whether it is fresh, make sure the answer is truthful but informative of the fact that the food is of the highest quality. Remind the customer that the meal is prepared by your chef in your own kitchen. Good frozen food is always more healthful and better tasting than food that used to be fresh.

One of the more hostile expressions in American life occurs on menus: "No Substitutions." It is the antithesis of a fine restaurant.

You will find that some customers have been lied to for so long by other restaurants, especially in the big cities, that they refuse to believe you even when you tell the truth. I went fishing on my birthday one time, after our restaurant had been open for more than a year. That evening, having caught the limit of Pacific bluefish, I proudly announced to the dinner guests that the fish was absolutely fresh, since I had caught it myself. This was too much for one of our local patrons. "Don't hand me that baloney," he said emphatically. "Bring me the pork chops, and don't try to tell me you slaughtered the pig."

I learned a good lesson that day. Had I kept my mouth shut about catching the fish, he might have discovered for himself that the delicious, delicate flavor of truly fresh fish does not have to be advertised—nor can you fake it. If it is fresh and is prepared expertly, it shows.

Precooked Frozen Food?

If you create a small restaurant that specializes in preparing meals of high quality that compare favorably with those cooked at home, you will want to avoid the many precooked and "factory"-prepared frozen items that rarely meet the above criterion. You cannot imagine the number of food items on the market that are touted as labor-saving, "high-profit" movers. Did you know that you can buy an extruded frozen roll of hard-cooked egg about 12 inches long? This labor-saver must be used with a special slicer, but it does produce a set of uniform egg slices for garnishing salads. And each slice looks as though it came from the widest part of the egg. Who knows what has been added to it to make it extrude uniformly, slice evenly, and keep in the freezer for up to a year?

The most flagrant example of this kind of food merchandising I have ever experienced personally occurred many years ago at a famous old seafood restaurant in Malibu, California, which had a lovely view of the Pacific Ocean surf. The place had always been known for fresh seafood, so I ordered stuffed prawns. When they arrived, I was appalled to discover that they were breaded, prefrozen, and deep-fried; they lay limply on the plate and tasted as if they were left over from the previous year. But the price of the dinner was set as if it had been prepared in the restaurant's own kitchen.

A number of old-time favorites—including scampi (which are not breaded!), chicken Kiev, stuffed boneless trout, stuffed pork chops, veal cutlets, and, believe it or not, lobster bisque—have lost their distinction under these circumstances. You may decide to revive their popularity by preparing them properly.

Your Wine Stock

The ability to judge young, great wines and to lay them down under properly controlled conditions can be the difference between a good wine list and an outstanding one. If your restaurant becomes known for its gourmet food, a great wine list will bring the best clientele to you rather than to a competitor whose food may be equally good.

Restaurant owners sometimes eat at a competitor's place just to keep tabs on him. A chef I knew always served his competitor a lousy meal—not because he didn't like him, but because he wanted to keep him complacent. He reasoned that if the competitor found out how good he was, the other place would try harder and improve.

If you are interested in wines, owning a fine restaurant gives you the chance to have a lot of fun at wholesale prices. But do not place yourself at the mercy of a wine salesman who cares more about popular brands than about how the wine tastes. If you are to have a distinctive wine list, you must rely primarily on your own taste. You should supplement your judgment with that of your knowledgeable clients; ask them to suggest wines and taste them. Occasionally, you may also find that a local liquor store owner or salesperson is a connoisseur of fine wine; such an adviser can be invaluable. If you are a neophyte, you should begin now by reading books and newspaper columns about wine; there are many good publications from which to choose, especially if you want to learn more about the wines of a particular region.

Until recently, viticulturists were in the dark about the origins of the Zinfandel grape. It was suspected, but not proved, that it had originated somewhere in Europe, perhaps near the Mediterranean. Through the efforts of a forensic botanist, DNA analysis of the Zinfandel grapevine shows it to be a descendant of the Italian Primitivo grape. This shows that you can always learn something new that will be of interest to your patrons. (Who knew there was such a thing as a forensic botanist!)

You will be limited by the amount of capital you can afford to invest in wine, by the amount of proper storage space you have, and by the price range that your patrons will accept. The wines produced in your region may have some limitations, but if you are really interested in wines, you should make connections with suppliers of premium wines from both local and faraway wineries. Or you may be able, once you are well established, to travel to and make contact with smaller and medium-size wineries. There are successful wineries in all parts of the country, some closer to you, whose products will be of use to you. Go there and taste and discuss their specialties, if you live nearby.

Your initial wine list should be prepared with the assistance of at least two knowledgeable salespeople from suppliers that distribute fine wines in your area. They should be selected for their knowledge of wine and for their understanding of fair pricing policy. Beware of the ones who tout high profits from certain brands. Gouging the wine-drinking public is a no-no.

Your list should include a selection of three house wines (red, white, and rosé). The rest of the wine list should offer a number of higher-priced, better-quality red, white, rosé, and dessert wines served in bottles labeled by the vintner with the name of the grape variety (or variant name) used in making the wine. The label often contains the year of harvest as well. These varietal wines are referred to in this chapter as vintage wines, to distinguish them from house wines. However, this distinction is not always clear in practice. For example, a number of restaurants offer Cabernet, Merlot, or Zinfandel, varietal wines, as one of their red house wines. Many more restaurants (and wine bottlers) offer bottles labeled with generic names that are reminiscent of areas of Europe, rather than denoting the grape variety; some even have a vintage year on the label. But the generic names for American wines bear little or no relation to the classic grape varieties used in Europe for those types of wine. These generic names include burgundy, chablis, champagne, chianti, claret, moselle, port, rhine, sauternes, sherry, and tokay, as well as other proprietary names devised by the large wineries to sound like premium varietal wines for mass market sale.

Start with a modest selection and build your wine list slowly and carefully. If you can afford it, it is nice to have a small selection of the finest wines and champagnes in the high-price category. Such wines may be requested by special customers on special occasions. They need not be included on the list, as long as someone in the dining room is well prepared to discuss wines with the customer.

The House Wine

Your house wine is an important part of your offering. In the past it was purchased in bulk quantities, such as gallons or half-gallons. But as the number of wineries has exploded in the United States, you are now more likely to be offered modestly priced wines in case quantities bottled in fifths or liters. A house wine selection provides a good wine in amounts less than a bottle, or offers the equivalent of a bottle of vintage wine at a lower price. House wines are normally served by the glass, half-liter, and liter.

If you view your house wine as merely a cheap offering, you do a disservice to the average patron who relies on your good taste. Your choice of a house wine should allow you to serve a wine you are proud of at a moderate price. I recommend that you choose a dry wine, to satisfy the restaurant patrons who favor dry wines with food. You can accommodate the sweet wine drinkers with an inexpensive selection of fruitier wines, especially rosé and light whites.

If you become known for having an excellent house wine, the volume of your sales as well as the time saved in not going through the cork-pulling ritual will make up for the perhaps smaller unit profit built into your house wine prices.

Staffing and Personnel Management

YOUR BASIC staff consists of you and your partner; your servers and other optional dining room help; and your kitchen help, dishwashers, and cleanup and maintenance crew. There are some small restaurants where cleanup each night is done by a combination of the servers and cooks. This is not ideal; it is too demoralizing to have to clean thoroughly after an already hard day of serving or cooking.

From a management standpoint, there are two key positions in a restaurant. One owner should be in the kitchen, preferably as chef or assistant chef. The other must be out front in the dining room, at or near the cash drawer. There are no easy substitutes for these two people, except possibly a dedicated relative of one of the owners. In the current business practice, however, it is necessary to find, train, and ultimately trust a skilled stand-in for at least one day each week. With a limited menu, it should be possible to entrust the kitchen to an assistant chef, thereby allowing an owner-chef to enjoy a shift at the front end, greeting customers. A dedicated and experienced server can also readily step into the front-end manager's position for a shift, especially on a slow night.

Hiring

You must expect all positions on your staff to have periodic turnover. (None will have a higher turnover than dishwashing.) If you are properly prepared, however, you should have less trouble finding replacements than the larger, less personal restaurants. Yours should be one of the best places in town to work. A small restaurant's staff is like a family. If it is a happy and prosperous one, many will wish to be adopted into it.

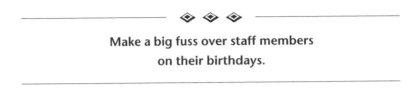

**Make a big fuss over staff members
on their birthdays.**

All hiring must be the result of a two-step process. First, each prospective employee must fill out a short application. Then, each applicant must have a personal interview. The first step provides you with a record you can file for future reference; it becomes a part of your minimal personnel records. The interview gives you the most direct evidence for deciding whether the person will fit into your "family."

Employment Application Card

You really need very little information about each prospect that is bona fide occupational qualification data. Strictly speaking, the applicant's name, address, telephone number, date of application, and previous experience, with references from former supervisors, are all you can expect to get that is of real value. You will not need to know marital status or Social Security number until after you hire, when you must figure out the withholding allowances for tax purposes. Detailed personal health information is not permitted to be requested on such applications. And most states no longer require restaurant workers to have a current Food Handler's Certificate, which was a way to screen all such employees for tuberculosis and other communicable diseases.

You will be very interested in whether your prospect lives close enough to the restaurant to be able to get to work easily. You will also want to be able to reach him or her by telephone at any time; therefore, at least an answering machine is essential. Other vital data might include age (if alcoholic beverage service is involved), whether the applicant has adequate personal transportation, what hours of employment she is willing to accept, which positions in the restaurant she is willing to accept, whether she smokes tobacco, and whether she speaks any for-

Sample Employment Application Card

Front

Mr. ☐ Ms. ☐		Date
Phone		
Address		
POSITION DESIRED		

PREVIOUSLY EMPLOYED BY	How long	Reason for leaving
1.		
2.		
3.		
4.		

DUTIES	Full or part time	Supervisor's name
1.		
2.		
3.		
4.		

Back

REMARKS:

PERSONAL REFERENCES

Name & address	Phone	Relationship
1.		
2.		
3.		

eign languages. Each of these items may be relevant to your operation or personal preference for employees.

Previous Employment

This information is of greatest use in deciding whether your prospect should be hired as a trainee or an old hand. You may wish to avoid the problems of training a server from scratch, although there are managers who want only workers who have not yet established any bad habits. Grace and personality are more important than years of experience, but a little restaurant experience is better than none at all. You should qualify the experience listed on the application by asking detailed questions about the kind of place the applicant worked at, and the nature of the duties he or she performed there. The reason why employment was terminated at each place is a useful bit of information, especially if it is a local reference and can be followed up. If you are already familiar with the other restaurant, you will be better able to evaluate the reasons your prospect gives for having left.

Experience and Traits to Look For

What experience counts? Someone who has worked in a variety of restaurant positions, including dishwasher, will have a better understanding of any job you have available. You may find out more about an experienced waitperson by the questions he or she asks you, rather than the other way around. Often, an applicant will have already asked a lot of questions of one of your employees.

**Do not hire anyone who will make customers
lose their appetites.**

Basically, you are interested in whether the applicant has worked in a restaurant with a similar atmosphere to yours, and whether the responsibilities assigned were relevant to your operation. If you need a lunchtime kitchen assistant to make salads and sandwiches and also work during the day shift to prepare for the dinner service, it would be best to find someone who has done those tasks elsewhere. However, someone with table service experience in a place that served sandwiches and salads would be far better qualified than another applicant with no restaurant experience at all.

Some of the characteristics to look for in restaurant workers are honest comments about past difficulties or mistakes, quickness, a pleasant voice, and a look of cleanliness. It is difficult to describe the characteristics of people whom you will not want to hire to serve your customers, but there are a few that are so obvious that I list them only as an exercise. The following list of B.F.O.D.s (bona fide occupational disqualifications) for any restaurant worker is strictly unofficial:

1. Unpleasant voice

2. Hostile attitude

3. Stubbornness

4. Slovenly grooming

5. Chronic body odor

6. Alcoholism

7. Diseased teeth

8. Extreme obesity

9. Skin eruptions or disease

10. General poor health

Keeping a Reference File of Applicants

The application card should have a space on the back in which you can note answers to your questions as well as other observations you make during the interview. By using a 3 x 5 or 4 x 6 index card, you will make it easier to keep a file of applicants who can be called on short notice. The file should be culled every six months or so to weed out old applications. This is a process that can easily be done if you have such data in electronic files on a computer, but a manual system works quite well and never crashes. If you choose to have a more sophisticated interface with the public via a Web site, you can also use it to advertise your employment openings and invite applicants to submit their resumes via e-mail. None of this is really necessary, and there is no substitute for face-to-face interaction as part of the hiring process, but it could widen your selection of experienced personnel. And it might be cheaper than running a want ad. Once you are known for your food and service, a simple Help Wanted flyer posted near your entrance may bring the very person you hope for, very likely a relative or friend of a good customer.

You may believe that you have no openings at the moment a good prospect comes in to apply for a job, but that situation can change overnight. It is only fair to state the facts to an applicant, but it is to your advantage to have the application on file for later reference. If your reputation as a fair and honest employer accompanies your excellent name for food, you will undoubtedly be visited by many qualified people. Be sure to determine whether the applicant is currently employed at another local place. If so, ask how much notice is expected before the new job could be started. That will give you a clue as to how much concern the person has for the problems of running a restaurant.

The Probationary Period

Every new hire should be on a temporary basis until initial impressions are confirmed. The probationary period may be as short as a week or as long as a month, but it should be made formal. Perhaps the starting pay can allow for a small raise after a month's probation. With servers, look during the probationary period for signs that spell later trouble. Does the new server arrive late or continue to forget simple instructions? Are there frequent mistakes in noting quantities and prices? Are all food and beverages accounted for on a completed check? Any unpleasant personality traits will show up at your tables under stressful conditions. Ask your regular customers for their candid opinions of the new person.

Selecting Servers

When screening applicants, look carefully at the handwriting or printing on the application. If the chef would not be able to read it easily, perhaps you should disqualify the applicant. I recommend that both the chef and the dining room supervisor take part in interviewing and evaluating server applicants.

You may be located in an area where there is a good selection of both male and female serving people. There are regions of the country where more female applicants appear, but you are subject to the equal employment opportunity rules that apply everywhere. As the United States continues to lose traditional manufacturing jobs, your openings in the service sector will be in demand. It is the service that counts. Your personal preference, restaurant style, and décor will help determine whether to use a costume, distinctive uniform, or other identification for your servers.

A klutz should not work in a restaurant.

It may be permissible for you to discriminate on the basis of physique, hairstyle, or other personal features if you can establish it as a bona fide occupational qualification for your restaurant. For example, if, for your Victorian-style dining room, you decide to dress your staff all in top hat and tails, striped pants and spats, and short hair parted down the middle, any applicant who is willing to comply with those rules has a right to be considered and hired, if she is otherwise as qualified as anyone else you hire. If you tried to limit hiring to blondes, you would have to show why a server in a blonde wig was not qualified, if it came to an actual case. I strongly advise you to consider and hire on the basis of gracefulness, personality, and a friendly face.

Hiring a Chef

The best small restaurant operation is one in which the creator of the selections served is also a principal in the ownership, with or without a partner. That premise underlies much of what I have written, but it does not rule out employment of a head cook or even a full-fledged *chef de cuisine* to serve a discerning clientele. The owner who also can cook and manage a kitchen can serve as a backup or even as assistant chef or cook, as the case may demand.

In almost any arrangement, including a partnership, there may well come a time when a head cook or chef must be hired, either prior to start-up of the place or as a replacement for a departed chef-partner. The need to replace such a key staff member could stem from something as commonplace as an extended maternity leave or recuperation from major surgery. What appears below applies as well to a head cook as to a formal chef.

A thorough search and background checks are essential when filling the primary position in the kitchen. Especially when time is short, it will pay for you to try to limp along for a little while without a replacement by using your existing staff, perhaps with a temporary replacement, to allow time to find and interview the best choice. Since your regular staff likely includes a cook who fills in for your regular chef on his or her day off, the ongoing training and development of such a person to cover an unexpected absence should always be a high priority.

If your patronage has increased significantly since you first opened, in all likelihood you will have been contacted by, and have on file an application from, a promising sous chef or cook who lives in the area and wants to join your successful team. You may also be acquainted with a retired chef in the area who gave you advice when you first started. Such resources should always be cultivated for emergencies, for vacation coverage, or just for professional association and friendship. Personal recommendations are desirable if they come from a reliable source, but do not overlook other potential sources such as publications directed toward restaurateurs or gourmet cooks. Check the "seeking employment" ads in food industry magazines and wide circulation newspapers. If you know a local food or restaurant critic who likes your place, you might consider approaching him or her in confidence for possible leads.

Any individual to whom you entrust your kitchen, and ultimately your reputation, must be someone with whom you share a reasonably common approach and philosophy about serving the public. The more experienced the candidate, the greater the potential for understanding and agreement about key issues. But, be warned—there is a higher incidence of alcohol abuse among chefs and cooks than among the general population. The job is uncommonly stressful and it is understandable that a talented and hard-working person may carry the unwinding and relaxation process too far, to the point of alcoholism. A credit check may provide a clue, but a reference check question should directly address that issue.

A qualified candidate will have credentials and a work history, references, and perhaps even a local reputation. For example, a sous chef or other specialist may be known for her desserts or pastries, and may be ready to take over as the head of your kitchen. Or, a line cook under the management of an executive chef in a large operation may tell you she has the desire and the commensurate experience to be the mainstay of a smaller restaurant such as yours, but with the same high standards. All such claims must be thoroughly followed up and investigated. It may be appropriate, when considering a less experienced applicant or a recent graduate of culinary arts training, to arrange for the candidate to prepare a few menu items, such as appetizers, entrées, and desserts, to see what results. If you are considering a currently employed chef or sous chef, you or a trusted friend should visit the restaurant where that person cooks, sample some items, and have a discussion of that menu and operation during your interview.

Remember that the boss of the kitchen must have leadership skills in addition to food preparation and artistic talents. The chef not only supervises kitchen operations, but he or she also plays a major role in managing and interacting with your food suppliers. Even if the owner retains final control of major menu and food cost decisions, the chef is your main hope of controlling waste, spoilage, and the *esprit de corps* of your staff. Try not to hire a tyrant. But even the best chef will get angry under certain circumstances, so the key is how well and quickly he or she gets over it.

No matter where you are located, your suppliers' sales representatives may prove to be a good source for finding a replacement chef. If you trust a rep's discretion, he or she may be able to suggest someone suitable. But be prepared for your competitors to spread the rumor that you are in trouble, once they get wind of your situation from those very same sales reps, who will be the first to notice that your chef is already gone.

If you are located in an area with many fine restaurants, there is likely to be a culinary arts training academy nearby. Legitimate academies often have an internship program that you may have already tapped when you needed extra help. If so, you should keep track of any especially good interns from prior years whom you remember personally or who now work at another restaurant that you frequent on your day off. Likewise, the training cadre at the academy will be another source of recommendations about candidates, such as former students who are between jobs, or even former colleagues. There is always turnover in the field due to failed business or incompatible personalities. The latter case requires caution and good intuition but could offer a feasible opportunity. Remember also that a business could have failed for reasons other than uninspired cooking, so you will have to sort it out when interviewing an unemployed prospect.

At a minimum, your interview discussions with any candidate should get into specific details beyond the obvious ones related to your particular menu items, past employment responsibilities and experience, and credentials and references. You should ask about the candidate's expectations for timing and interface with servers, what style of kitchen interactions your existing kitchen staff will be expected to conform to, and how the candidate has dealt in the past with different personalities and emerging situations in the kitchen. If you already do extensive large party or catering events, whether on the premises or off site, that aspect of your operation requires a crucial area of expertise that you should probe. There are many such topics for an interview discussion that you can derive from other chapters in this book. Make a list and ask all candidates the same set of questions.

Be prepared for an experienced candidate to look over your kitchen setup and to suggest or ask for changes. There may also be preparation times, weekend operating hours, or holiday periods that overtax the chef's time and energy and that a candidate will ask you to limit, supply extra help for, or change from your prior practice. Do not vacillate or equivocate on such issues. You must either stand firm and insist that an offer depends on acceptance of such conditions, or negotiate in good faith to implement changes that are reasonable. The worst thing you can do, after making promises and hiring a good candidate, is to renege on a promise or try to weasel out of part of your agreement. Loyalty goes both ways. If you cannot stick to your agreements, you had better learn to cook.

When you find an excellent candidate, you must be prepared to offer a salary commensurate with his or her experience and within the range of the local job market. If the hiring occurs before you start your operation, you are justified in setting a reasonably long probationary period that includes an appropriate salary increase or bonus when certain pre-set goals are met. The higher the base starting salary you can offer, the longer you can set the probation, if you have any initial doubts.

Finally, when your chef is not an owner, you will have to pay for what you get. The more success you achieve, the greater will be the chef's expectation for monetary reward. At the outset, this is often arranged by setting yearly goals upon which a bonus amount can be based. But the base salary will have to be competitive to ensure that you can make a deal, since the candidate is also counting on your performance to be part of the success. The ultimate objective over time is to achieve a mutual commitment to the success of the restaurant. Such discussions will occur throughout the tenure of your relationship, but it is not wise to have your initial agreement and understanding remain an oral arrangement. The hiring process should culminate in a written contract that reflects every important facet of what you both expect. Do not expect either a good contract or circumstances, however, to produce a permanent solution. You must both be realistic at the outset about the possibility that the employment will someday come to an end. You must reflect this reality in contract wording to cover whatever can be anticipated as the basis of termination. Aside from a standard clause covering termination for cause, you should cover amicable separation requested by either party. Minimum notice and arrangements for working with a replacement should be covered. Handling of an earned but unpaid bonus should be appropriately established. The duration of the contract and the manner of extending or renegotiating the agreement should reflect the fact that you really don't know each other yet. Once long-term compatibility and mutual satisfaction have been achieved, you can reward excellence with a longer contract and more money, if profitability warrants it.

The downside of having to employ a chef is that, while working hard to get used to each others' styles and hoping for the best outcome, you still may find that even after a spectacular beginning, the new hire may not reach your expectations. You will have to be firm in your resolve to make the hard decision to begin a new search for the right person to be your chef.

Training

I firmly believe that at some time in each person's restaurant career he or she would benefit from experience washing dishes—preferably as his or her first experience in a restaurant. It is a good question to ask prospective servers: "Have you ever been a dishwasher?"

Training your staff to do things the way you want them done is one point on which you will have to be firm. There may very likely be someone in your employ who has more restaurant experience than you do. That is very good, if she has learned that each place does things differently. Suggestions should be welcome, and often may be useful to you. But your style is your style. Some issues will simply relate to the policies that you want reflected to the customer. Other issues may directly affect profits, such as the size of a portion. If the cheesecake is to be cut into 24 pieces, that means that your waitress cannot decide to cut it into 20 pieces because she likes to serve bigger portions.

> **The bearer of compliments to the chef should deliver them as soon as possible, especially when something else has gone wrong. But a minor complaint ought to be handled without involving the chef, if possible. It should be reported at a time when it won't make the kitchen mood worse.**

The chef is the key to training servers on attitude. A sensitive chef will suppress outbursts of temper at the peak of the dinner hour by limiting him- or herself to a grouch or two. The pressure of daily performances will affect even the best of restaurant staffs. A good crew always returns to pleasant relationships after the rush is over.

If you want to see something really funny, watch the expression on the face of the chef when a waitperson is acting up. As soon as the order has been picked up and the server has turned and started out to the dining room, the chef will exhibit some of the most amazing grimaces imaginable. But when the chef is having a snit, watch your best server as he comes into view of the diners. If he is really good, no matter how bad he feels or how difficult a time he has had in the kitchen, the customer will see only the most benign look of equanimity. Maybe there is a hidden clue. Hire unemployed mimes, and your success is assured.

Staff Meetings

As in any business, it is essential to the success of your operation to hold periodic staff meetings. Arrange them at the most convenient time for most people, even if some have to make a special trip. The meeting will provide an opportunity for the staff to suggest ways to improve the operation, as well as for you to give everyone the chance to react as a group to your ideas and rules. Keep staff meetings short and hold them infrequently, but make each one count by dealing with real issues.

Feeding the Staff

Your rules for staff feeding will require some strict understanding. As a general rule, you should insist that your employees arrive at work ready to work, not to eat. You must specify which food items may not be served to the staff unless offered by the chef or owner. Staff people should eat at the staff table at the appointed time. If they join friends at a customer table, they should first take off aprons or other "on duty" items of clothing; otherwise, the public will assume they are still on duty and resent their inattention.

If you serve alcoholic beverages, it is imperative that you control their consumption by the staff. That means no one drinks on the job, and no one gets a free beer unless one of the owners offers or approves it. (There will be times when a glass of champagne makes the difference between making it through the shift with a smile or offending a good customer.)

If business is slow and you want someone to walk into your restaurant, just sit down to eat. Within five minutes, someone will interrupt you.

You are feeding your staff for your own benefit, not theirs. It keeps them conveniently on the premises, it provides quick energy when they need it, and it keeps the "family" happy. If your chef is wise, the staff meals will be selected and timed to provide an additional reward for good effort. Sometimes the real reason why a dishwasher or cleanup person will continue to work for you is that he can eat better at your place than at any other.

There was a famous restaurant in Morro Bay, California, whose owner was one of the most gracious hosts in the business. He was a connoisseur of fine wine, and his wine list reflected it. After closing, when he and his staff sat down for dinner, he was known to pop a cork to introduce the serving people to his latest wine acquisition, or to refresh their taste of an old standby. As a result, his servers were able to recommend wines intelligently to their dinner guests. And their own dinner was a time they looked forward to at the end of a hard evening's work.

Dishwasher Blues

"Where am I going to find another dishwasher at this late hour? We're going to have a horribly busy night, too!" At some time in your restaurant career you will find yourself speaking or hearing these words. It might seem that the job of washing dishes is not an important one. But there is really no job in a restaurant that is less important than another, excepting the chef.

Washing dishes is not an easy job, yet it is considered in many restaurants to be a task fit only for semi-competents who can't do anything else. Managers with that attitude have no one to blame but themselves if the job is done without grace and care for the dinnerware. Dishwashers usually deserve more pay than they receive. One way of making up for that is to provide more fringe benefits, such as an extra meal or extra time off. In the end, no dishwasher, whether good or bad, will stay long at the job. If a dishwasher is really clumsy or slow, he must be replaced as soon as possible. If one is quick and careful, give her a raise, be nice, and maybe she'll stay past Labor Day. We have hired both male and female dishwashers. It is too hard a job for anyone who is not long on stamina. A lot depends on whether the dishwashing area is kept cool and whether the kitchen staff is able to interact well with the dishwasher. The job is made easier by busing tables so that the bus trays may be emptied efficiently in groups of utensils, rather than making the dishwasher pick out napkins and silverware from between plates.

The wave of immigrants who have dispersed to almost all corners of the nation makes it likely that you will hire a dishwasher who may have little or no ability to speak and understand English. If no one else in the kitchen speaks that person's language, there are several important steps you should take upon hiring. First, be certain that the probationary period and whatever conditions you impose have been understood at the interview, presumably explained to the applicant by whomever accompanied him or her. One of those conditions should be that the applicant must learn sufficient English in the next months to meet your requirements. For that to happen, you will be doing that employee a favor by arranging for some type of tutoring. Even if you have a foreign speaker already on the staff, the new employee needs to speak and understand everyone else's instructions. You can schedule a raise to be earned by passing a rudimentary language test. If the immigrant is fortunate to be sponsored by a community group, such tutoring may already be in progress, but you need emphasis on the language and terms used in your workplace. Ask that the tutor phone you or stop in to talk with you. Your job offer is a crucial step in the life of a new resident. Make the most of it. And be patient, but firm.

Scheduling Part-Time Workers

It is quite likely that your staff will include very few full-time people other than you and your partner. The weekly work schedule is an important factor in keeping your part-time workers on their toes. The server's schedule can be a crucial determinant of tip earnings and of status. (Yes, Virginia, there is a pecking order in every restaurant.) You will have to use the weekly schedule as a tool to try to even up everyone's chances of earning good tips.

Unless you serve only dinner, you should schedule your most experienced servers for the dinner period. The busiest nights should be rotated among them all. Normally, tips are better at dinner, and smart serving people will ask for a night schedule. But if you have a good, reliable staff established for dinner, and you have an opening for a daytime server, do not make the mistake of promising the applicant that he or she will be able to move to dinner work. Any really excellent daytime server who would enhance the dinner staff can always be offered the promotion later.

If your business is seasonal, or at least varies from day to day, you will soon learn the pattern. You must know the times that are likely to be busy ones and arrange your staff schedule accordingly. Be certain to keep daily records of the number of people served at each meal. These records are crucial to the next year's planning. Make notes on holidays or special events in your town that bring more business your way. Any extrapolation from the past, however, is imperfect. There will be days when you have too many people working to handle scant business. If you can, send someone home early. Or perhaps you can arrange for someone close by to be on call.

Do not allow substitutions in the work schedule without your prior approval. When you schedule a waitress for a busy weekend and you know that she would rather spend it with her boyfriend, be prepared to go to the limit on the issue. If someone else is able to fill in for her, and it is convenient for you, fine. But double shifts make for exhausted servers, and you must have final control.

It boils down to one hard fact: When you work in the restaurant business, you do not usually get the same holidays that other people take. If you need the job, you work when you are scheduled, and you do not call in sick unless you are. If someone cannot accept the schedule, he cannot work for you. (Obviously, there are reasonable exceptions and alternatives. But you can go crazy trying to please everyone.)

Quit or Dismissed?

The work schedule may also be used to try to get a slipping performer to quit so that you don't have to dismiss him or her. If business is slowing down, the poorest performer is usually given the fewest hours to work. If the person cannot afford to work so few hours, he will sometimes look for another job. If he complains, that may be a good time to suggest that he try to find a better-paying job.

This method is not entirely satisfactory, from a number of viewpoints. It may just make the problem worse for a while until you take the bull by the horns and fire the guy. In the long run, it pays to do it honestly. If the employee no longer has the desire or has not developed the skill to do the job the way you and your customers want it done, tell him to find another job. If possible, give notice or pay in lieu of notice. Do it without recrimination or arguments to try to justify the unpleasantness. Even though it is not easy for a nice, creative person like you to fire someone, you are most likely doing him a favor. If you cannot stand to have the person working for you, it will eventually affect him badly, or it might contribute to your business failure. So do a favor for the two of you and move the unsatisfactory employee out.

Summer Resort Labor

If you happen to be located in a summer resort area, Labor Day weekend is an important milestone in your business cycle. It signals the end of the busy season. It can also be the point at which you are ready to collapse because two weeks earlier half your summer crew decided to leave for their own vacations.

At our place, if anyone was found to be smoking pot on the job, he no longer had a job, unless he could prove he had glaucoma, a serious eye ailment relieved by cannabis. A few of our staff thought they were catching glaucoma for a while, but it is not a communicable disease.

It works like this. Along about May, you will be accosted at all hours by eager young people who want summer jobs. When asked, they will all promise to start work immediately after school is out and stay on until after Labor Day weekend. Do not believe it. If these folks have been in school all year until early June, work hard all summer, and have not had any vacation, by mid-August they will begin to get very dissatisfied with life. Some will leave it at that. Others will quit and take a vacation, now that they have some money saved up.

There are two ways to handle the problem. One is to try to hold off starting them at work until just before July 4th and to tell them to take two weeks of vacation right after school lets out, even if they have to borrow the money for it. The other method is to hire them with the strict understanding that their hourly wage will depend on whether they stay through Labor Day weekend. That is, if they expect to be paid $9 per hour, they will receive $7 of it on each payday, with the remaining $2 per hour payable at the end of the summer. That way, if they quit early, you will have some money with which to hire someone else in a hurry or to pay your loyal crew an extra bonus for working harder. This method may not be possible if you are paying minimum wages. Check with your state labor department first.

Cleanup and Maintenance

S O YOU HATE HOUSEWORK and you're thinking of opening your own restaurant? Be warned, there is no end—and there are no shortcuts—to the cleaning and maintenance of an operating restaurant. The only thing that really cuts grease is elbow grease. If you are acquainted with a compulsive cleaner, hire him or her and pay a bit more than the going rate.

Daily Cleanup After Closing

Each day the kitchen should be cleaned completely following the last meal served for the day. (This simple rule must be understood at the front desk when late arrivals plead to be allowed to eat after you have closed.) Once the kitchen is closed, all food is immediately put away and cleanup begins. If it is not done until the next morning, you allow the vermin army to establish a beachhead from which further assaults will be repulsed only with great difficulty.

If the chef is the one who must clean up each night, and she does not have competent help, either the chef or the restaurant will not last more than a few years. A good chef, however, will clean up in small ways all day and conscientious food preparation assistants will continually wipe and gather up garbage around the work area. Do not allow the development of an attitude that "the cleanup crew will get it."

Traditionally, cleanup begins with the cleaning of the griddle, if you have one, by rubbing it with a block of volcanic pumice and cooking oil. The release of the natural sulfur in the griddle block is a subtle signal that the day is coming to a sometimes exhausted close. A small putty knife completes the job of scraping the pumiced oil from the corners of the griddle. There is nothing like a shiny griddle to make the chef feel good in the morning.

Kitchen surface cleaning is accomplished with the aid of a plastic spray bottle filled with a mixture of water and vinegar. It is applied liberally and wiped with a clean towel. There are commercial solvents of all sorts that maintenance supply salespeople will try to sell you, but it is hard to beat the cost-effectiveness of vinegar water. Beware the stainless-steel polish that is oil-based. If it smells like something you would not want to have your food taste of, forget it. It was made for looks, not sanitation.

Constant wiping, scrubbing, and shining of kitchen surfaces—vertical, horizontal, and otherwise—is the only sure way to keep them clean. The main horizontal surface in the kitchen is the floor—and it is thus the recipient of everything that doesn't get caught by the ceiling, walls, shelves, and equipment. It's just like at home, only much worse. The floor supplies the dirt to be tracked everywhere else in the restaurant. Sometimes the maitre d' will wonder whence came a trail of cantaloupe seeds through the dining room. A visit to the disaster scene in the dish room would have answered the question. Clumsy John is working this shift and he can't seem to find the center of the garbage pail—only the edge.

The floor should be swept several times a day just to keep it from getting too grungy before the night cleanup crew gets to it. The kind of floor surface you must have to meet the health code was discussed in chapter 4. Almost any material used to create a hard, nonskid floor requires periodic renewal to keep it functional. Be certain that your cleaning agent, grease cutter, and other substances used daily do not cause pitting or breakdown of the kitchen floor. The old standby for restaurants used to be ceramic tile. Now even concrete floors (which are so devastating to your legs and feet) can be surfaced with a type of plastic-based deck paint developed for boats. It allows for excellent cleaning results without being too slippery, and it can be renewed quickly.

Any type of food slicer or processor, whether it is a big attachment to a mixer or a simple vegetable slicer, must be completely taken apart and cleaned after every day that it is used. Meat grinders and electric slicers such as those used in a delicatessen have crannies that you can't begin to imagine unless you have personally taken one apart to clean it of food particles. I recommend you do so several times so you can check on your cleanup crew.

Periodic Cleaning

The restaurant health code usually requires that certain kinds of maintenance be performed on a regular basis. The same logic applies to the cleaning chores under your direct control. You should impose a strict periodic cleaning schedule on every piece of equipment used in the kitchen. (See page 175.) The most important of these are the grease filters in the exhaust hood and the grease interceptor (or trap) in the sewer line. The drain lines from sinks require attention to abate grease buildup, especially if they run horizontally for more than a few feet before dropping into the main line.

Garbage disposals in sinks that grind up food waste create a special problem for drain lines. You are much better off saving all your edible garbage for someone who raises pigs. Get in touch with your local 4-H club to find out about nearby pig farmers. If you are in a city where no one will contract for daily pickup of your edible garbage, or if you are in a municipality that prohibits the use of grinders with private sewage disposal systems, you must be prepared to hold your garbage in tightly closed containers, to prevent animals and vermin from getting at it, until the garbage service picks it up.

Periodic cleaning and maintenance are also essential for automatic dishwashers, the hot-water booster and heater, and the ductwork for the kitchen exhaust system. The blower fan is another item that can suffer grease buildup. The rooftop grease pan that is sometimes installed below the exhaust blower air outlet must be cleaned and checked regularly. Many a restaurant fire has occurred because the ductwork was ignored for too long, even though the kitchen was kept clean. For ease of maintenance, the ducts should be exposed, if possible.

If your restaurant is so small that you have decided against installing an automatic dishwasher, you will be using a sink with a disinfectant rinse to wash your kitchen equipment. But this does not remove grease film as well as does the 180°F rinse in an automatic washer. Therefore, I recommend you try to arrange for a service that operates portable steam-cleaning equipment. Have them come around several times a year to steam clean your exhaust grease filters and other kitchen equipment thoroughly. It will probably not cost too much if the service is not too far away or can come regularly for several customers. You may have to contract for a year's service.

Cleaning Out the Grease Trap

The location of the grease trap can present an odor and temperature problem, as discussed in chapter 4. Although it must be cleaned more often, the great advantage of a small grease trap, as opposed to a large one, is that the cleaning job is accomplished in a relatively short time. You must determine the schedule for cleaning by your observation of the need, the type of menu you have, the habits of the preparation crew in draining grease in the sink, and how much business you have. If possible, it is best not to dispose of grease in the sewer line at all, but to pour it into a container, seal it tightly, and put it out with the trash. Wipe out as much grease as possible with paper towels.

**Treat the person who repairs your refrigeration
with sweet gentleness.**

The best way to clean a grease trap is with a clothespin and a modified metal ladle-like utensil originally designed for lifting large pieces out of a deep pot. The ladle has a shallow bowl, with holes to allow the liquid to drain. But this type of ladle always has a circular bowl, and your grease trap has square corners. So you just make the utensil workable by bending up two edges of the ladle to create a corner with two adjacent lips at right angles that will fit nicely up against the sides of the trap. Using this simple device, you can ladle up the semisolid grease at the top of the trap without taking the dirty water beneath it. When you

CLEANING SCHEDULE

DAILY

    Griddle and range

    Steam table

    Sinks, drainboards, and backsplash

    Microwave oven

    Dishwashing machine and drainboard

    Kitchen floor

    Appliances and equipment surfaces

    Restroom sink, toilet, mirror, and floor

    Dining room carpet and floor

    Tables and chairs

    Coffee machine

WEEKLY

    Grease filters

    Refrigerators

    Grease trap

    Windows

    Spot clean carpet

    Wash all dispensers for salt, pepper, sugar, honey, syrup

    Clean all shelving

    Clean all crevices in shake mixer, drink dispenser, milk dispenser, toaster, slicer, coffeemaker, hot fudge machine, syrup dispenser, etc.

    Polish woodwork

PERIODICALLY

    Freezers

    Dishwashing machine nozzles and reservoir

    Storeroom

    Hidden corners in kitchen and behind equipment

    Vacuum dust on vanes of refrigerator compressor units

    Wipe down walls

    Steam clean accumulated grease in ducts, etc.

    Drain lines in sinks

open the trap and find a lot of grease and not much water, that means you are not cleaning the trap frequently enough. The clothespin is for your nose. If you insist on watching your cleanup person do it, you will need two clothespins.

Side Work

"Side work" is an activity that any experienced server performs when not otherwise busy. It refers to the 101 items around a restaurant that need to be wiped, cleaned, and polished. It is not busywork. The accumulations of dust, greasy film, and general spills and residues in the most unlikely places must be constantly sought out and removed. Side work fills the interstices of a shift with activity that justifies having two servers working even though one and a half servers could easily handle the customers.

Your servers and dishwashers are your first line of defense against the relentless advance of grease buildup. It will happen anyway, despite your best efforts. This is why most health codes require periodic repainting of restaurant kitchens, and also why all kitchen surfaces including the ceiling must have a hard, smooth finish. (Ever try to wipe down a tongue-in-groove pine ceiling?) Corners can collect enough food for an army of roaches, and you are not the commander-in-chief of that army. Just let one word get around that someone found a cockroach in one of your dinners and you will have a more difficult time eradicating that story than you will getting rid of the pests.

Dust is a kitchen phenomenon that does its work slowly. You must vacuum it away from the grid on the condenser of each piece of refrigeration. These parts are usually hidden from view behind a panel so the dust is not blown on the food, but you had better find them. The shelving in the kitchen may be all stainless steel, if you had a huge budget, but dust can be wiped away just as well from plain pine boards that have been properly treated with a hard finish such as varnish or polyurethane plastic.

The Dining Room Floor

Caring for your floors other than the one in the kitchen may require some special equipment. If you have carpeting in the dining room, it should have a short, hard nap, and it should be vacuumed daily with an upright commercial machine such as a Kirby. All sorts of stuff will be ground into your carpet, so it is best to choose a color and design that will blend in well with the spots of salad dressing, raisins, sour cream, strawberry preserves, hot fudge sauce, coffee, steak fat, soy sauce, and cooked carrots. The table area where you usually place the high chair for infants will be a special carpet maintenance target. The only way to avoid having to replace the carpet too often is to use a can of spot lifter on each evening's or each week's spills. (It is good to have a couple of cans of spot remover around anyway to take care of occasional spills on a customer's clothing. It works quite well on most fabrics.)

If your floor is not carpeted, you will use a mop and buffer, or perhaps you will have a kind of surface that does not require buffing. Uncarpeted flooring can be quite noisy unless it is on a cement slab. Your décor may not call for carpeting, but it is the floor covering that looks best while it lasts and it is almost as easy to maintain as a washable floor. It hides wear better than most other surfaces.

Restroom Maintenance

Your objective is to keep the restroom from being a problem to your customers. They should be even more pleased with your service after a visit to the restroom than before. A few simple rules will help achieve that goal.

The restroom should be stocked with a hand soap that is germicidal, not just sweet-smelling. Get the concentrated liquid kind used in hospitals and dilute it with water. I prefer liquid soap dispensers over powdered or bar soap. They are less of a mess and easier to keep clean, and there is less waste. Folded paper hand towels in dispensers result in a basketful at the end of the day, but they are less unsightly than the continuous-roll cotton toweling that hangs, covered with dirty handprints, like a towel at a boys' camp. You may have the money to invest in one of those noisy hot-air blowers with the adjustable nozzle you can turn up to dry your face. Does anyone ever really dry his face with one of those things?

Keep your bathroom supply dispensers full and in good operating order. It is unlikely in a small restaurant that any dispenser of paper or soap will run out during any single mealtime. Therefore, you will avoid trouble if you check and replenish supplies before each meal service. A patron who is forced to use a paper towel instead of toilet paper will very likely cause a plumbing overflow. In such cases, it is nice to have more than one restroom available so that the one with the problem can be temporarily closed until the floor is mopped.

The other potential problems with restrooms revolve around illness and discomfort. If a patron is drunk, sick, or unhappy with someone at the table, he or she frequently ends up in the restroom. And you may be left with a mess to clean up. It helps to have a cabinet or closet designed right into the restroom for storing the cleaning supplies that will make the job easier and quicker. I believe that the more your restroom design and décor remind the patron of home, rather than an institution, the less likely he is to make a mess of it. Keep it simple and familiar.

Advertising and Public Relations

T HERE IS ONLY ONE sure method of advertising for the small restaurant. When you serve an outstanding meal to delighted customers, they become an effective and consistent source of advertising. As such people leave your front door, do not hesitate to encourage their assistance. As an old restaurant adage has it, "If you liked it, please tell your friends. If you didn't, please tell us."

Getting Your Name Known

Your building is an advertisement. The tasteful use of lettering and color, whether in the form of brilliant flowers, a mural, a mosaic, or any other attractive artwork outdoors, should send a message from you to anyone who goes by.

It is worth directing some effort toward establishing good word-of-mouth recommendations in your community, whether it is a small town or a neighborhood of a big city. It is not complicated. After you have been open for a few weeks and your routine has gelled, invite some local businesspeople to enjoy a complimentary meal at your place. If possible, do it for an organized group, such as the local motel association; otherwise, invite managers individually. The targets of these efforts should be people most likely to be asked where in town there is a good place to eat. They include managers of motels, gas stations, tourist-oriented businesses, executive secretaries in industry, local politicians, and people who occupy chamber of commerce information desks. Remember, too, the local office of the automobile association. Pour your house wine generously and serve a lovely meal. Your investment will come back to you tenfold.

> **I despair for the traveling public each time I am told, "We have been on the road for three weeks now, and this is the first meal we have had that makes us feel as good as we do at home. It was delicious."**

Public relations boils down to a few simple precepts. Be honest in your advertising, in your dealings with customers and creditors, and with your employees. When a mistake is made, give the other person the benefit of the doubt by assuming at the outset that there was a failure to understand. Apologize first for your mistakes, then compensate. Answer all your mail promptly and with style. Assist those in trouble if they come to you, even if it is not on the menu. Send some hot soup to the sick child of a traveler at the motel. Give the person who is down on his luck an hour or two of work picking up the trash in your parking lot and sweeping the sidewalk, and pay with a good meal and a few bucks. Public relations is simply having empathy and acting on it in a way that serves others. It won't work if you view it as a chore or quid pro quo.

Build Up Interest Beforehand

Plan your advertising campaign well in advance of your opening, so it can be carried out in a reasonable and economical way. The first ads might even appear as "ticklers" during the last few weeks before you open. For several weeks before the opening of the Grey Fox Inn, the following ads appeared in our local newspaper with our fox logo:

First week: a tiny display ad saying just, "The Fox."

Second week: a small ad saying, "The Fox is coming."

Third week: a larger ad saying, "The Fox is coming soon!"

Fourth week: a large ad saying, "The Fox is here!"

The last ad contained a full description of the restaurant location, hours, and type of meals available.

Display Advertising

When you advertise in a newspaper or magazine, design your display ad thoughtfully. Use an easily recognizable visual feature such as a logo or special lettering for your name and aim for readability with a clear, appropriate typeface, a few lines in a bolder type, and plenty of white space. It is not difficult to learn what the newspaper people have to do to prepare your ad for print. If you are going to advertise regularly, but will change part of the text periodically, you should understand what is easy to change and what cannot be changed readily just before the deadline. In general, plan to use the same framework and art in your ad each time it appears, changing only the text portion within. If you have a logo or picture you will often want included, make sure you understand in which type of electronic file format it is kept. Find out how to ensure that your original copy of the artwork can be backed up or scanned for current and future advertising needs.

A one-column-inch ad is one column wide by one inch high. A four-column-inch ad may be one column wide by four inches high, or four columns wide by one inch high, or two columns wide by two inches high.

Always try to arrange to check a proof of your ad, or at least check the wording by telephone after the ad is laid out. Mistakes will be made, in any case, despite everyone's wish to avoid them. If you cannot check the copy beforehand, be sure to do so as soon as the publication hits the street. If there is an error, you can at least limit it to that one issue.

Some newspapers have a restaurant page where most such ads are concentrated. Whether or not to place your ad there is a question for

Our Place

Seafoods and Fancy Country Fare

Brunch every Sunday
11:00 A.M. to 3:00 P.M.
$12.95 per person

Dinner served from 5:00 to 10:00 P.M. daily.
Reservations accepted. Call 666-555-4444.
See www.ourplace.com for more
interesting information about us.

Uptown Center, Someplace, Pennsyltucky

empirical results to answer. Try it both ways to see whether one part of the newspaper yields more results than another. Some papers will ask you to sign up for three months of advertising on their "business directory" page and will promise to run a feature story about your restaurant on that page once during that period. This whole idea, which presents advertising thinly disguised as news, is not high on the list of good newspaper practices. But so many papers, especially weeklies, do it that you might as well take advantage of it. If you can write well, perhaps you will even be allowed to write the feature article yourself.

News Items and Reviews

A real news item about your place, in any case, is always better than an advertisement. If there is a restaurant guide or critical review section in your town or city newspaper, get in touch with the editor of that feature. Write up a succinct and interesting news release—perhaps including a recipe for one of your chef's specialties—and set up an arresting photograph to go with it. In a big city, the restaurant critic will be thoughtful enough to wait until you have settled in a bit before visiting, but your news release might fill an empty space on the food page. If you are in a small town, the weekly paper may run a story about your opening just out of courtesy. And you can usually get your press release into one of the free "advertiser" papers that are delivered to every doorstep in many neighborhoods.

A good display advertisement is both elegant and specific.

If you are located in a small town, the following comments are directed specifically to you in relation to your small-town newspaper. The economy of a small community is a wondrous and fragile thing, and one of the principal links that holds the whole entity together is the community newspaper. Steady advertising revenue is absolutely essential to the survival of any paper, especially one in a small town. Decide realistically what you can afford, but advertise regularly. And pay your bill each time it is presented. Especially in a restaurant, you will get business in return for such good habits.

The interdependence of people in a small community is what caused this country to evolve its abiding character. There is a rebirth of recognition of this going on all over the nation as a counterforce to the impersonal relationships of the megalopolis. It is a reaction, as well, against the corporate balance-sheet bottom-line mentality that spawned, for example, the epidemic of franchised "fast food" farces claiming to be restaurants. The small restaurant and other individual enterprises such as local craftspeople, merchants, and newspapers are a vital part of the counterforce. If you open your restaurant as a way of living in a small town, your obligation to the small-town newspaper is clear. It doesn't matter whether or not you agree with the publisher's politics; the children of your staff and the children of the advertising representative deserve to live in a vital small town with a good restaurant and a good newspaper.

Reaching Tourists

When you consider advertising in a magazine-type publication oriented toward visitors to your town, city, or region, you must be very certain of the effectiveness of the format and the distribution method. For example, a brochure placed directly in each motel room, passed out to each automobile rental customer, or mailed directly to convention registrants is more likely to attract visitors than the same item sitting on a counter or rack in the lobby. The total number of such brochures printed is less meaningful than the number actually placed in the hands of prospective customers. Also, take a look at other publications the same outfit has produced before you place an ad. Sometimes the quality is so poor that your being included can do more harm than good.

The cost of this kind of advertising can be quite high. Do your best to see that your ad has high recognition value and is placed in an appropriate spot in the publication. As a general rule, an ad should return at least 110 percent of its cost in profit dollars to make it worthwhile.

The Internet

Even if you do not have your own Web site, there is almost certainly one or more that are to be found by tourist net surfers looking for your town. The local chamber of commerce or hotel and motel association will usually have one. There are two ways for you to make use of such "bulletin boards." If you have your own Web site, arrange for the chamber of commerce or other site to display a link to your site. Make sure that the link works by testing it and ensuring that it has no misleading or confusing information. Even if you have not opted to create your own site, other sites such as one for a group of restaurants catering to tourists can list your restaurant name, address, phone, and perhaps a short description. You may already have an affiliation, such as being a chamber of commerce member, or you may have to contribute a modest fee to get your place listed.

The Telephone Book

The telephone book is a form of advertising that requires advance planning. Find out the deadline for listings in both the white and yellow pages relative to your opening. You cannot have a white-pages listing unless you have a telephone. If the deadline is in October, but you will not open until January, it might pay to install the restaurant phone in your home or in an office near your location, just to get the listing. When calls come in, you can explain that you plan to open in January and request that the caller try again then. When you finally do open, the telephone can be transferred to the restaurant.

You can use the same technique with the yellow pages. If you can afford a display ad, use the space to describe your restaurant and advise the reader to call for directions. The monthly charge may be worth being in the book for the better part of the year that you intend to open. After your first year, you can decide whether you really need a display ad or whether the alphabetical listing under Restaurants, with a few extra lines of description, will suffice. The yellow pages may have another restaurant list broken down by nationality of cuisine. Place your listing there also, if appropriate.

Your Menu Is an Ad

Place copies of your menu at strategic locations such as motel desks, car rental agencies at the airport, and other places that guide the traveler. Don't overlook bulletin boards in such places as laundromats, supermarkets, and miniature golf courses. And don't hesitate to give a menu to anyone who asks for one; charge a nominal fee if necessary.

When you travel, do not rely on billboard signs. The best way to discover an excellent small restaurant is to visit a local business establishment and ask the owner or salesperson where in town he or she goes to eat.

Billboards

I can think of no instance except for major emergencies in which the use of billboards is better than a large display ad in a widely read publication, or a spot on television, or in any medium that does not spoil the look of the countryside and the architecture of our cities. Posting bills on smaller kiosks at appropriate visitor centers would serve the people who never look at other media and would not contribute ugliness on such a grand scale.

Having said all this, if outdoor advertising space is available in your area at a reasonable cost, you should consider its use at least until you are better known and established. But get the best sign painter you can find to design your ad for you. Perhaps you can cooperate with other businesses in your immediate area to place a multiple-services sign at an opportune location.

Radio

Radio advertising can be quite effective if the announcer has firsthand knowledge of your restaurant. When an announcer talks about the luscious scampi he had the other night at your place, he can actually make people's mouths water. The personal rapport attained on both FM and AM radio can have a striking effect, if done well. But you must arrange to have the disc jockey or station manager eat at your restaurant before he or she performs the advertising spots.

Early in his baseball career, New York Yankees catcher Yogi Berra had to supplement his income by working in the off season. One year he worked in a restaurant, the one he was referring to when he uttered his famous quip, "Nobody goes there anymore; it's too crowded."

Most radio spot commercials are set for 15, 30, or 60 seconds, and broadcast during a particular time slot on predetermined days. If you contract for longer periods, you may get a price break or better choice of time. To prepare a properly focused radio campaign, you must become familiar with local programming formats and audiences. Ask the station representative for verified listener profiles when preparing to select your station or stations. You can have several ad scripts prepared and used in rotation or to fit the day of the week and time of day. Be certain to listen to your ad or have the final scripts sent to you before you approve the broadcast.

The FM stations that pipe music into offices and department stores may be of help to you in drawing local employees. The type of music played on the station pretty well determines the market you will appeal to. If you wish to attract classical music lovers to your gourmet hideaway, weekend and evening programming is a good time in which to concentrate most of your spots. If you are using a station piped into offices, advertise on weekdays between nine and five. And do not overlook a popular station in a nearby city if your area draws people from that city for recreation or shopping.

Talk Shows

Radio talk shows are a means of spreading word-of-mouth recommendations for dining out. On this sort of program, people call in to a restaurant reviewer who discusses places to eat in whatever locale is requested. Urban radio stations have developed this format to the delight of astute listeners, who hear about countless places that they might otherwise never discover. Each format is different, but these reviewers cannot be bought. They give their own judgments of the places they visit, then they allow callers to voice their own reactions on the air. You can have a friend help you get some notice by calling in to report on your place. But you had better be good—if you are not, it will be reported later by other listeners. So wait until your service and timing in the kitchen are down pat.

Podcasting

In 2004, an Internet phenomenon emerged that makes use of MP3 players such as the iPod. The ability to create an audio file for downloading to an MP3 device makes possible what can simply be described as homemade radio shows. Such free "broadcasts" can be subscribed to online. As of this writing, the ease with which a show of that sort can be created is problematic, but it is very likely to improve with time. The technology already exists to allow you to sit at your computer with a microphone to create voice material and combine it with music, even live music recorded at your restaurant when you invite local musicians to perform. Your teenager may already be listening to podcasts. If your restaurant is appropriate for such audiences, check it out. You could have your teenager help you get your name and special talents to a select audience. You even could get mentioned by bloggers.

Advertising Follow-Up

Do not leave to conjecture the effectiveness of your advertising campaign. You must ask your customers how they happened to come to your place; don't rely on them to volunteer the information. Keep track of what sources are most effective and spend your advertising dollars accordingly. If you must make a choice from among several local papers, you might try making some sort of special offer redeemable with a copy of the ad. Place the ad in two different papers. (The back of the cut-out ad will be different for each paper, so you will be able to tell which ad brought in the most customers to your restaurant.) You may find that both papers are closely read and do equally well in bringing business, or you may be surprised at the difference.

Public Relations

The Chamber of Commerce

Join the local chamber of commerce. They will officiate at your "grand opening," which takes place at your convenience after your real opening. A photograph of the ribbon-cutting event always has the possibility of making the newspaper. You will probably be too busy to participate in chamber of commerce activities at first, but as a member you can have a voice to protect your business interests if something threatens your particular area or restaurants in general.

Community Theater

If you have the good fortune to be located in proximity to a small theater, whether amateur or professional, you should take pains to support the group's efforts by taking out program ads, placing posters for their productions in your lobby, and doing whatever else you can afford to do. There is a special feeling for such support, among both the theater-going public and the troupe itself. You can offer special incentives to the theater patrons to eat at your place by tying the theater ticket stub to some discount or complimentary course. You may be able to cater a cast party. If the group is professional, you may even employ cast members as servers, while they are waiting to be discovered.

Charity

A multitude of local and national charity appeals and other solicitations will be directed to you during the year. Although you cannot possibly contribute to them all, you can do certain things. You can offer meal gift certificates to a selected few for use as door prizes or raffle prizes in fundraising campaigns. This sort of public contribution should be narrowly focused so as to limit your expenditures yet bring you the goodwill they engender.

If your restaurant is dependent on transient customers, one of the tricks of the trade on a slow day is to have all employee vehicles parked in front of the place.

Contribute to what is of genuine interest to you. Do you have children in school? Support school activities and limit other contributions; take an ad in the high school yearbook or support parent organizations involved with youth activities. Perhaps senior citizens, the blind, or the mentally disabled are your special interest. Whatever you do, use your business as a moral asset to put back into the community what you have taken out in another form. You may think you can't afford to contribute. In truth, you can't afford not to.

The Guest Book

A guest book offers two advantages. It gives credence, of a sort, to what people have heard about your place. They see written evidence, created by people like themselves, of how good you are before they enter the dining room themselves. In this way, the remarks in a guest book at the front desk serve as a sort of "point-of-sale" advertisement.

Second, it allows your guests to comment indirectly but effectively to the chef. It may not always be easy to take, but it is valuable. If you are doing things well, the remarks will reinforce your beliefs. If there are shortcomings, they may show up in the comments, or in the absence of comments. (Make sure your guest book has a column headed "Remarks.")

Prices and Profits

Y OUR ENTIRE EFFORT now focuses on whether you can make a financial success of your venture. Even if you are independently wealthy, your restaurant should show a profit for the time when you decide to sell it.

Setting Menu Prices

Dinner Prices

The price of dinner at your restaurant can be determined using the following rule of thumb: Multiply the wholesale cost of the "protein" portion by three, four, or five. Four is the norm. The multiplier you use will depend on what else is included in the dinner price. If you serve soup *and* salad, a relish or other appetizer, potato or rice, and a vegetable, then the higher factor may apply. If you serve a complete dinner, including a beverage and dessert, you will be more likely to offer smaller portions of the main dish to avoid waste, and this may keep the price down. If you mainly use an à la carte menu, where the patron gets to choose the side dishes desired, you may wish to price the main course a bit lower. Your competition may limit your flexibility.

The wholesale prices of fish have risen as consumption increases and supplies dwindle. The multiplication factor has always been higher for a fish dinner because the spoilage rate is much higher and the labor of preparation is just as great as for most meat. If you are charging $15.95

for a dinner with a 12-ounce portion of meat that costs you $5.90 per pound wholesale, you may very well decide to charge $17.95 for the equivalent portion of fresh fish that costs you only $4.90 per pound. More likely, you will serve a larger portion if the fish is not a rich variety, such as salmon or swordfish, in the high-price dinner category.

Most restaurant critics will categorize your price range as moderate, expensive, or medium (in between). You should decide the lowest price the public ought to pay for a dinner at your restaurant, and then try to have at least one menu selection at that price. If you set your median prices in the $14.00 range, then a customer should be able to get a good dinner at your place for $11.00 to $18.00. Add the price of a nice bottle of wine, tax, and gratuity to see what it will cost two people to have dinner.

The majority of American middle-class restaurant patrons would rather pay a little bit more for food that is really fresh, tasty, and beautifully served than pay an average or "bargain" price for mediocrity.

Nowadays, many menus price everything à la carte. If your main course includes a small soup or salad, your menu should be clear to differentiate the price of the full dinner from the à la carte prices for larger portions of soup and salad. In a small restaurant on a busy night, you should expect to serve just soup and salad to a couple who may also share one of your great appetizers for their main course. Set your à la carte prices accordingly. The hidden benefit when a table wants just the main course without appetizer, soup, or salad is that you make your normal percentage profit, but you will get the table that much more quickly for the next party. Many people, you will find, are interested in the full dinner menu.

The end price of the typical dinner should add up to what you and your local customers consider to be a fair value for the amount and quality of the food. If you are facing stiff price competition, you will have to be satisfied at first with a lower profit until you are established.

There are many ways to ease the burden of eating out for people who appreciate fine dining but are on limited budgets. My favorite restaurants offer several types of appetizers that, with a salad or soup, are a perfect main course to satisfy the smaller eater. You can serve "specials," in limited quantities, on the nights or days that are usually slow or at times when the less affluent are willing to patronize your place. Or offer a price inducement to people who come for a meal early, when you would normally not be crowded but your staff must be on duty anyway. For example, you might offer a discount on the second dinner for a party of two Monday through Thursday between 5:00 and 7:00 P.M. Although the profit on both meals is reduced, the increased cash flow pays the overhead, keeps the servers from getting bored, and makes your suppliers happy because your orders tend to fluctuate less.

Discount Affiliations

One of the side effects of the ubiquitous use of credit cards has been the proliferation of "clubs," or affinity group discounts. The major inducement for people who use such cards is the offer of a substantial discount taken off the check total, sometimes as much as 15 or 20 percent. Another benefit is a guidebook that lists participating restaurants (and hotels, rental car agencies, etc.) in faraway cities.

None of these features carry any easily measurable benefits to you. Your decision to participate in such schemes must be made on the basis of whether other factors provide you with a real incentive, such as the availability of short-term cash advances offered by such membership groups.

A person who simply hasn't enough money to leave any tip at all should either eat in a less expensive restaurant or order less. In Europe, he would have no choice: A 15 percent service charge is automatically included in the final price.

In the past, to receive the discount, members had to carry and present a special card. That is no longer a requirement because of the powerful database capacity, the transaction speed, and the credit card processing that can automatically check for discount membership affiliation. It works like this. Upon joining, the patron specifies to the "club," such as "Rewards Network," which credit card account(s) will be used for payment whenever a participating restaurant is visited. If the restaurant offers a 10 percent discount to such members anytime, or on Sundays through Thursdays, or for their first visit each month, the credit card meal charge is flagged by the credit card processor. That monitoring is completely transparent to the restaurant staff, to whom the payment appears like any other transaction. The applicable discount is handled at the time the transaction is posted by the credit card issuer and takes the form of a refund applied to the balance in the same way as for a return credit on merchandise. The meal charge transaction and the refund are both identified on the monthly bill by the restaurant name, date of service, and posting date.

The real issue here is not the convenience for patrons, however, but rather what such membership discounts cost you and whether they really increase your volume of business. There is no question that they will significantly reduce your profit, because the "club" extracts a much higher "discount" from you than what is offered to the diner member. You will probably be giving up all your profit for that meal and more, if the fee is as much as 50 percent of the food and beverage total on the check. Remember that even if the check total subject to the "club" discount does not include sales tax or the tip added on the credit card charge, there is still a hidden cost. That is, your credit card total on which you pay the processing fee, nominally 3 percent, is artificially inflated, even though a large percentage of that sum represents what the "club" has extracted from you. For example, if you agree to participate and you receive $5,000 in cash up front, over time you will end up repaying $10,000, as the diners using their "club" discount rack up food and beverage charges. In a small restaurant, it can take a while to sell $10,000 worth of meals to members.

Several factors affect your decision whether to participate in such schemes. Do you have a better source for getting operating cash? How much new business from members can you expect to be attracted to your place; how many days of the week would benefit if the promise of new patrons proves true; and for how long must you commit to forgo your hard-earned profits to pay back the up-front cash? You should get a report from the "club" showing the ZIP codes from whence your diners came. It will soon be very clear whether your local patrons or visitors from afar are using the discount. If they are primarily local, and most of your competition does not offer the discount, your decision whether or not to remain in the "club" will be somewhat easier to rationalize. It is clear that if you do join, you will probably not want to offer to "club" members other discount deals via giveaway coupons or the like.

Portion Size

Portion size is psychologically important in many parts of the country. If you are serving ranchers, loggers, or other hard-working people, you may wish to offer seconds to accommodate their tastes without producing too much waste with ordinary customers. But even that offer is ticklish to administer. You may have to have the server handle it rather than putting the announcement on the menu.

I was asked many times why our menu did not offer a smaller portion at a reduced price. Some restaurants do make this a common practice, especially with steaks or prime rib of beef, for which it makes very good sense. But the price of the meal depends on more than the weight of the meat portion. A large percentage of the price must pay for labor and overhead. Obviously, these factors are exactly the same for each meal served, regardless of portion size. Most patrons do not realize this and are puzzled if the reduced price of a smaller portion seems still too high.

Breakfast and Lunch Prices

Breakfast and lunch prices usually do not have to reflect as many courses as dinner. Therefore, the price of a sandwich may end up being set other than by a rule of thumb based on the wholesale cost of the protein source in the sandwich. It is better to charge a little more and serve a sandwich that makes people at the next table sit up and take notice. If you add some little side dish that does not cost too much to prepare, but offers a contrasting taste and a pleasing presentation on the plate, set the price to cover the added item. Junk foods, such as soft drinks, are always higher-profit items. I am in favor of charging high prices for them to discourage people from ordering such poor foods, especially for children. Fresh fruit juices, on the other hand, are already expensive; anything you can do to hold down the price on those items will make you more popular. Your lunch or breakfast trade and the competition from other nearby places will, in the long run, determine your price range for these meals.

The popularity of coffee drinks that require more than just brewing has diverted attention from the American habit of offering unlimited coffee refills in restaurants. No one seems to expect a second latte or espresso for free. If you open for breakfast, you may find your small place filled with coffee drinkers who order nothing else. They sometimes take up space that would otherwise be occupied by bigger spenders. Your coffee policy is a personal matter. But you must consider several factors when you set the price of a cup of coffee. It might not be so bad for the price to be too high for the "coffee sitters." On the other hand, it might not be wise to turn them away on the days when they might actually eat.

In the United States, coffee is the only restaurant commodity in wide demand for which most places charge a flat price regardless of the amount consumed or ordered and left uneaten. In Europe, coffee is a high-priced dessert item served by the cup or pot. When the first portion is empty, you must order and pay for another.

It is reasonable to have a minimum charge per customer on busy days. Do not be ashamed to make a good profit. You will have to work harder for it than almost anyone else I can think of.

When setting the prices of side dishes or à la carte items, take pains to do some simple arithmetic. If your regular menu offers a combination of items, make sure the sum of the separate items' prices slightly exceeds the price of the combination. For example, if you serve a cup of soup with a sandwich and a beverage as a lunch special for $7.75, the separate cost of the same amount of soup and the same sandwich and beverage should be at least $8.50. If homemade pie is $2.95 per serving and a scoop of premium ice cream is $1.25, then pie à la mode should be $3.95 or less.

Extra Charges and Specialties

There will always be customers who desire that some item not on the menu be added to a sandwich or salad. It keeps life from getting too routine. Make sure you post a menu in the kitchen so the staff will know the prices of such extras. When setting these prices, be sure to consider the added cost of labor in breaking the normal preparation routine, as well as the size of the added portion. Be reasonable and fair to both yourself and the customer. A small restaurant in our town antagonized many customers by deciding to charge an extra 25 cents to heat a sandwich. It was a foolish move, because it annoyed even those who never asked for a hot sandwich. People are willing to pay extra for a slice of avocado, which they know is expensive, spoils quickly, and involves labor to prepare. But they rightly resent being charged for heating in a microwave oven.

When you set the price of a sandwich, consider the size of the slice of bread on which it is normally served. If someone asks for a substitution of, say, your sourdough bread, which may have significantly larger slices, it could require 40 percent more filling to keep the sandwich from appearing skimpy. You might have to charge more if you cannot obtain different kinds of bread with similar-size slices. But do not nitpick. Some costs will simply average out over the year.

If you serve some very attractive specialty that is prepared in your kitchen, such as a special dessert or soup, or any other unique dish, be sure to charge a fair price that is not too low. Your actual labor costs may not be as great as the customer assumes and your ability to ensure quality is inherent in the preparation, perhaps with a secret family recipe. If necessary, adjust the portion size to keep the price reasonable. One way to promote your special ability or idea is to offer small free samples to certain customers when you first introduce the dish. Soon the rest of the town will hear about it and come to try it.

Validate Your Profit Margin

Once you have some period of operating data to analyze, you must validate your initial menu pricing by looking at factors related to your gross volume of sales. In the past, if an operation could keep the combined cost of food and labor to a figure under 65 percent of gross sales, it was likely that a reasonable profit could be made after accounting for relatively fixed costs comprising rent, insurance, workers' compensation, utilities, and advertising.

The rising cost of many of the relatively fixed expenses, especially insurance, utilities, workers' compensation, and payroll taxes on higher minimum wages, now requires you to use a lower factor, i.e., a range of 53 to 58 percent, for the combination of food and labor costs. Your food costs will be dependent on which meals you serve and how much is made from basic ingredients. The more kitchen labor involved in preparation, the higher your labor cost percentage will be. If you take a strict percentage figure as a guide for pricing each menu item based on the cost of the ingredients and portion size, you will get a somewhat rigid measure of the validity of your menu prices. Other factors, however, may allow you to be more competitive but still achieve your overall profit margin goal. If you have a very popular item that outsells most of your other menu choices, the volume of sales on that item contributes a greater portion of your profit than other selections. That may allow you to price the popular item at a lower level than indicated by the cost of the ingredients. This is especially important for items with lower labor preparation costs.

When applying the profit margin analysis to your menu pricing, the following nominal percentages apply. For a low food cost operation such as a standard Mexican or Chinese restaurant, costs in the range of 20 to 25 percent can be achieved. For a menu based on quality ingredients and fair portion size, costs should range between 30 and 33 percent. If you are serving customers who expect large portions, such as for a western steakhouse, costs run to 35 percent or more. Labor costs are more variable, depending on whether the owner is in the kitchen, whether an expensive chef and staff are needed, and how much labor turnover can be tolerated. At a labor cost of 14 percent, turnover will be high.

If labor costs for overall staffing with no superstars can be held to 16 to 18 percent, the optimal 53 percent combined labor and food cost can be achieved, even at a 35 percent food cost. If your analysis results are outside such ranges, either your prices are too low for high-cost items, your portions are too large, or your volume of business is inadequate for your menu and staffing, causing waste and slack time.

Finally, in the past you could expect to hold your pour cost for alcoholic beverages to 21 to 23 percent. Anything higher indicated a lack of bar control. There are recent trends toward increased cost for distilled spirits. State budget deficits lead many to increase alcohol taxes. That can make it impractical to price a beverage at more than four times the cost of the ingredients. Your choices include seeking acceptable cheaper substitutes if they exist or getting used to a lower profit margin on that segment of your gross sales.

Price Increases

When you are faced with eroding profits due to wholesale price increases, there is a basic rule you must follow: Maintain quality and raise prices. Your customers will understand. Do not wait too long to reflect cost increases. If you do, you may find that the price adjustment will be perceived as too great. Smaller increases will be accepted much more readily, even if they are more frequent.

One side effect of raising prices is that you will have to alter your menus. Therefore, design your menus so it is not too expensive to print new ones each time you change prices.

Investment and Return

The initial investment to start a restaurant from scratch in a location that has not been equipped as such may come to as much as $600,000. You may do it for less, but you should have enough reserve cash to cover the rent for nine months to a year. If you are able to find a partially equipped location that needs little renovation, you may be able to start with a lot less cash. But a good location is crucial, even if the initial cash requirement is high; you will recover your investment.

Regardless of location, reserve capital is necessary to cover the likelihood of your making some costly mistakes during the learning and start-up period. You should plan on replacing at least one key piece of used equipment, which will break down within a month or two after you open. Unexpected new public building regulations may require some unplanned cash layout. Even if none of this occurs, you must be able to protect your overall cash and psychic investment in case some fluke circumstance temporarily affects your business. For example, just after you open at a very good spot on a main road, someone may take a notion to begin a nine-month-long street-widening project two blocks away. The ensuing dust, detours, and delays may divert traffic away from your place. Don't be discouraged. Those construction workers have to eat somewhere, and they might come in if you visit the foreman to talk about your problem. (You may be able to get a "loss of business" insurance policy to cover such an eventuality, if you think to ask beforehand.)

If you have more like $850,000 to $1,000,000 to invest, you should try to purchase your own building. Negotiate that option, if it is a possibility, in any lease you sign—before your business and reputation are well established and the landlord raises the price.

What can you expect? You know that anything good will require you to put your heart and soul into it. It will take at least that, plus cash. The potential return is great personal satisfaction in your career, plus cash.

The annual return on your investment in a small restaurant is very likely to be small. If you are forced to borrow most of your starting capital at high interest rates, you will find most of your return going to debt retirement. That may be acceptable to you if you are building up equity in property that you are purchasing. If that is not the case, you should reconsider whether you can proceed without having the bulk of your starting capital free and clear. Most commercial lending institutions shy away from loans to inexperienced restaurant owners, and they are also reluctant to lend money on real property that has a single-purpose use, such as a restaurant, gas station, or bowling alley. If you borrow money from friends, they must be made very aware of the high rate of failure for restaurants and of the time it will take for you to repay the loan. Do not borrow amounts from friends or relatives that they are not in a position to lose. Spread the risk by borrowing smaller amounts from more people. But do not give anyone a piece of the action unless you incorporate and sell stock, making yourself the controlling stockholder. In a small restaurant there is never enough action for all the lenders.

Maybe you should go all the way and sell your home, if you have one, to raise capital. You won't be spending that much time there anymore, anyway.

The cash return can be figured fairly easily. Let us assume that you will have 25 tables, and you will serve two types of meals per day, six days per week, for 11½ months of the year. If each table serves an average of five meals per day, at an average price per meal of $12 ($9 lunch, $15 dinner), then:

25 tables x 5 meals x $12 x 6 days x 50 weeks

= $450,000 gross income per year

If your profit after expenses is 12 percent of your gross, you should net about $54,000 personal income before taxes. If the net profit must be divided two ways, you can see that no one is getting rich with a small restaurant, though you should also keep in mind that your food costs at home will be lower.

Serving seven days per week will add about $75,000 to the gross, netting an additional $9,000 before taxes. These figures may account for the fact that restaurants have the highest mortality rate of all small businesses. But what price do you put on personal satisfaction?

You may have fewer tables, of course, or a lower average meal price. The particular details of your price structure, restaurant size, and operating hours will all affect the gross income produced. But of even greater importance are your expenses and overhead costs. If you can combine low building cost with careful use of labor, you ought to be able to increase your net income and realize a net profit of closer to 15 percent. And if you can reach a level of quality and exclusivity that attracts the "carriage trade," you may even come close to an 18 percent net. But do not count on it, especially in times of inflation. If you decide to have only 15 tables and serve high-priced meals, your net profit may still be low because labor and overhead will represent a higher percentage of the gross.

There are other ways of netting a profit than in dollars, though. If you value shorter working hours, you may find it possible to survive on only one meal service per day, which is most likely to be dinner. Or you may be able to work only five days per week, just like average people.

Even better than that, if you are in the right location, you might work like mad for nine months of the year and take the remaining three to do the other things in life you want to do.

Restaurant patronage and cash flow fluctuate widely, especially if you are in a seasonal business area. The weather alone has a great impact on dining out. In our small town, where most people cook with electricity, the restaurants are jammed whenever there is a late-afternoon storm that causes a power failure. Since all restaurants use gas and the kitchen can be illuminated with a camping lantern, local people stream in to be fed, even in the semi-darkness of candlelight.

Because of these fluctuations, it is imperative that you keep close track of your expenses and intake on an almost daily basis. Each week you should have a pretty good idea of your food and labor costs compared to your income. You can easily approximate the fixed overhead costs for the month and assign a weekly amount for that. The cost of food should not exceed 30 to 35 percent of your gross income from food for the week, excluding state sales tax, if any. (The markup on alcoholic beverages is greater, so figure it separately.) Labor cost computation should exclude your own and your partner's draw. The percentage cited earlier assumes you do not offer employees any special fringe benefits for which you pay directly, such as health care insurance. It does assume that you will pay all the required state and federal benefits, such as Social Security and unemployment taxes. (Your minor dependent children are exempt from these requirements.)

Your fixed monthly and yearly expenses should not exceed 30 percent of your gross income. This covers:

- Rent or building payments, including property taxes

- Utilities, including telephone

- Fire and liability insurance, including workers' compensation coverage

- Linen service

- Maintenance and cleaning

- Regular advertising

- Permits, licenses, and special taxes

- Trash and edible garbage removal

- Office and administrative costs

- Cost recovery (depreciation)

- Miscellaneous costs for such things as soft water, gardening, extermination, special cleaning services, knife sharpening, bookkeeping, and dishwashing machine service

There will be seasonal variations in some of these costs, such as those for linens, utilities, and advertising. Your insurance premium may be adjusted each year following an audit of your gross sales and your payroll. Also, inflation will cause your overhead to rise each year.

Paying Your Employees

If you employ most of your staff on a part-time basis, you can probably pay the federal minimum wage to those workers who earn tips. Since kitchen people do not get tips, you will have to pay them more, except perhaps during a short initial training period. The prevailing wage for kitchen workers these days varies greatly by region and the availability of immigrant workers. Wages of $10 per hour, depending on the responsibilities assigned, are not unheard of, especially in a college town or similar limited job market with plenty of part-time labor available. The job market in your area is likely to force you to pay much more. (Federal law allows for trainees to be paid less than minimum wage for a short period, by prior written agreement, but important kitchen positions are not for a trainee.) Food preparation workers are rarely paid enough. Most restaurant employees know this and those who accept food prep jobs often expect to move up to server positions as soon as possible. A few small restaurants spread the wealth either by rotating people in both kitchen and dining room jobs or by pooling all tips and allocating them on some basis to all employees. Each system has drawbacks.

Employee compensation practices vary in the restaurant business. Nonunion wages for servers and buspersons are typically set at the minimum required by state and federal law. The busperson who does an excellent job usually gets 15 percent of the tips received by the server. You should establish a clear policy on that subject rather than rely on the good nature of your servers. Since the busperson has easy access to the tip on the table, a dishonest or dissatisfied busperson is intolerable. Even the mere suspicion that tips are being "ripped off" will immediately destroy the morale of the dining room staff.

Employee Meals and Benefits

The Public Housekeeping section of the Federal Minimum Wage and Hour Act is very clear about what you may and may not do in making deductions from employee wages. By prior written agreement, you may deduct from their wages the cost of meals and lodging. But you are not required to provide meals to your employees. If you do, you must pay Social Security tax on the value of the food, using a government-set amount for breakfast, lunch, and dinner. It is to your advantage, however, to provide meals to an employee who works a long enough shift to need a meal. In addition, since dishwashers are typically underpaid, it is common to provide at least one hearty meal to those workers per shift.

As mentioned earlier, it is a good policy that employees should arrive at work not expecting to eat immediately. After four hours, they should get a meal and a break. Federal law requires a half-hour break after five hours, unless the shift is over after six hours. The intensity of effort required at a busy restaurant often works against having time for even a bathroom break for periods of two or three hours. Common sense and caring among your staff members will establish reasonable practices for helping everyone get through the day without an accident.

Other fringe benefits, such as paid vacations, are not practical to offer when your staff has a high turnover. It is simpler to call the money a bonus and to pay it just before the restaurant closes for vacation. You can establish whatever incentives make sense for bonus eligibility, such as length of service. I have heard of restaurants that actively promote the sale of desserts or wine with bonuses as a reward for the server who can achieve above-average rates.

Group health and hospitalization insurance is nice to provide, but you may not be able to afford it along with workers' compensation coverage. Group life insurance is not necessary. However, you may wish to offer your people the opportunity to purchase their own health and life insurance at a group rate through the restaurant. (You will thereby get your own personal insurance at a lower rate also.) This usually requires the participation of at least 10 people for an entire year, but most small restaurants do not have a permanent staff of that size. You will also incur administrative costs. Check with a reliable insurance broker who has written coverage for other groups. Then compare the information with the coverage obtained by another small group in your area.

Losses Through the Back Door

I must now discuss a distasteful subject that has a direct bearing on your profits. People steal food from restaurants. Employees do it. Friends of employees do it. In a sense, even you are doing it, if you take food that your partner does not also take. Not only do the culprits take food, but, being connoisseurs, they may also wish to have a nice glass of wine or beer with it. If your food costs are exceeding 35 percent of your gross income and you cannot account for it through spoilage and analyzing your menu prices, then the food is going out the back door. No one is likely to break into locked storage, although it does happen. But the availability of keys to your storage and kitchen must be closely restricted.

Quiet security consciousness is the answer. If you deal honestly with your employees, losses of this sort will be kept to a minimum. If you catch anyone, deal with him or her swiftly and decisively. If you are a softie, you are being dishonest with yourself and your other employees, who depend on your staying in business for their livelihood. Change your locks occasionally.

Eating Is Still
"Low Tech"

BEFORE TOO MANY more years pass, many of your customers will not remember a time in their lives before personal computers and the Internet. What I referred to 20 years ago as "automation" has become commonplace in every important aspect of our daily commerce in the United States. People are willing to accept all sorts of inconveniences during power failures and other causes of automated system breakdown. When telecommunications fail, people cannot get cash from their automated teller machines and they accept that, if not happily, as a minor but temporary inconvenience. I remind you, however, that we also have paid a huge price for all this automation in the form of an insidious enabling of thieves to steal our virtual identities and, with it, our savings and good credit. There is no excuse for this situation. It is the direct result of the unwillingness of companies and the government to insist on good system design, because they have deluded themselves into thinking that it is too expensive. You do not have to make the same mistake.

Much of what I described and predicted in the 1983 edition of this book has come to pass. There are labor-saving devices in restaurants that eliminate almost all handwritten orders, checks, and records. Restaurants that have these devices probably do not have a well-practiced backup system to allow operation after a system crash. During a blackout, they probably have to close because they cannot prepare anything that uses electric power to cook, such as microwave ovens and coffee machines.

The following discussion is intended to reassure you that you can be successful in your chosen endeavor without becoming dependent on all the "automation" available. But you do need to be aware of all your choices.

What does all this have to do with serving good food? The enemies of quality include fatigue, waste, fraud, confusion, and inefficiency—all of which can abound when you have too much to do and too little time. Although smallness makes possible the managerial control necessary to maintain high quality, smallness alone does not prevent these enemies from invading your operation. Nor does it ensure that they can be driven out as you gain experience.

The development of wireless local network equipment allows a server at the table in a big restaurant, using a hand-held device, to enter and transmit orders that are printed out in the kitchen. I expect someday soon to see a news article about a disgruntled former employee figuring out how to mess up the kitchen operation by entering phony orders from a nearby doorway. Of course, this shouldn't be possible with a well-protected system design and security procedures where passwords are changed whenever someone leaves employment, but you never know.

A restaurant system, tailored to your needs, can offer you the means to neutralize the enemies of quality. You and your well-trained staff can assure quality without the aid of special equipment, of course, but to do so you need certain essential data about your operation, which take time to assemble. Your time is limited. The less often you examine your operation using these data, the more likely you will not discover the waste, fraud, and inefficiency that destroy your profit and thereby your ability to continue to offer excellent service.

So whether or not you believe you can afford one of the systems for restaurants, it is important to know just what is possible. It is well worth a closer look. The place to start is on the Internet. There'll be more on that subject later in this chapter, but first, for those who may not be systems-oriented, a brief tutorial follows.

Your Restaurant Is a System

Assuming that you have an ordinary operation, let us begin by looking at the point where the most important data are entered into your restaurant system. This occurs when a server takes a customer's order and writes it on the order form. Does it surprise you that I refer to your manual operation as a system? It *is* a system, you see, even if the only equipment you use is a pen or pencil, order pads, an adding machine, and a cash box.

Inputs

For the system to start, it needs to be told which specific food and beverage items the customer desires. The ancillary data written on the order are used for managing the process. They include how main dishes are to be prepared, table number, name of server, date, number of persons at the table, and possibly other information, such as whether special-offer prices apply. All this information is called "system input."

Timing

Separate copies of the multiple-part check allow transmission of the input both to the kitchen and to the source of beverages and side items, which may or may not be assembled by the server. A one-part order form requires the server to run back and forth or else to have a good memory. It is important that the kitchen staff know how far along the customers are in consuming the items that precede the main course. The chef must know when to start each cooked-to-order main course so all meals at a table can be served simultaneously, neither too soon nor too late. The chef must also consider the overall order of preparation for all tables so as not to make one party wait longer than others.

Outputs

Food and service are not the only outputs of your restaurant system. Another vital output is the bill presented to the customer. This bill is often the same form used for input, with the prices entered and totaled, including tax, if any. Some restaurants produce a guest check separate from the input order form, especially if they have a cash register with special printing capability.

System Problems

This is what can happen (and has happened) to the order form containing all that important input.

- If the handwriting is sloppy, it can be misinterpreted.

- It can become temporarily lost, stuck behind another order form or in a greasy crack.

- Additional items ordered can be omitted from the guest check, especially if the server can provide the item without going through the chef.

- When prices are inserted or the total added, sizable errors can occur.

- When checking the bill, the customer may find it difficult to read or understand it.

Solutions

In previous chapters, I have mentioned the importance of legible handwriting and a smooth and efficient relationship between servers and kitchen personnel. If there were a system that eliminated those problems by providing the following, would you use it?

- When the server enters data at a display terminal in the dining room, the exact order, including all ancillary information, is printed in the kitchen, where the chef and others can easily read it.

- Orders for beverages are printed at the location where they are prepared, also with ancillary data.

- Throughout the meal, the system remembers all information entered, including additions or substitutions.

- At the end of the meal, at the press of a finger, a straightforward check is printed in plain English, listing all items served with the correct price for each, and the correct total amount, including taxes, even if the tax rate varies with the type of item. The arithmetic is never wrong.

- The system records the method of payment—whether cash, check, or credit card—including the amount of any gratuity added on the charge slip.

There are obvious advantages to having all this information readily available to the staff members who need it. Elimination of arithmetic errors alone can have a surprising effect on profits. But some advantages of such a system are unexpected. One of the best is this: The server times the entry of data for each course according to the progress at the table. With this scheme, all items that appear on the kitchen printout are prepared as soon as possible thereafter. Thus, the chef is relieved of the stressful chore of juggling the main course preparation time for the entire restaurant. The timing of meal delivery is now almost entirely in the hands of each server.

Another advantage is that the server no longer has to memorize prices. Yet another is that at the end of a shift, upon pressing a few buttons, the manager learns the total amount of tips owed to that server from charge slips.

Management Aids

It is to the manager that such a system offers the ultimate time-saving advantages. Employees record their arrival and departure for each shift via the terminal, and from this input the system prepares payroll. Throughout a day's operation, information about any table is at the manager's fingertips for monitoring progress or for checking, for example, on whether the order for an expensive bottle of wine—or a second bottle of wine—has been entered in the system yet. If the manager wants to know how many meals of a particular type have been served, this information, too, is easily obtained, but only after the system has been put into the "manager's confidential mode" by use of a key or entry of a secret password by the manager. This mode restricts access to information that rightly should be available only to those with a "need to know."

Beyond the convenience of no longer having to go through the day's receipts, checking for errors in arithmetic, looking at the mix of meals served, and generally examining the day's results, the system gives the manager immediate access to specific information about the operation that is otherwise difficult to extract. The time thus saved can be used to better advantage in training employees, thinking of new ways to serve good food, or just enjoying the work.

Computers Never Get Bored

Regardless of how sophisticated a system you get or what applications you use with it, your managerial skills will be enhanced by the system's two main advantages: accuracy and speed.

Accuracy

All of your arithmetic calculations will be accurate. If the system reports that your gross sales for the week are $25,000, the amount will not be wrong because of a slip of the finger on your adding machine. If you ask the system to figure your labor costs as a percentage of gross sales, you can expect the report, no matter how often you request it, to show the correct amount, based on actual hours worked by your staff. Similarly, if you desire to know what percentage of gross sales each type of meal represents, and how this percentage compares with the relative cost of each type, you can rely on the accuracy of the reported figures, assuming that you have correctly entered the basic data needed for such calculations.

Speed

Generating the kinds of reports just described will hardly take longer than the time needed to switch the system to "confidential" mode, ensure that the correct report-generating program is selected, request the printout, and watch it emerge. The time needed to produce the same reports manually is normally so long that the small restaurant owner or chef rarely has at hand the vital information such reports provide.

The 23-year-old son of an Omaha, Nebraska, Vietnamese restaurant owner, whose younger brother had to translate orders written in English for their parents to understand, has created an innovative application to make operations easier. Tu Nguyen, while a student at the University of Nebraska, developed an application that translates the orders taken at the table in English via a wireless pocket computer and transmits them to the kitchen in Vietnamese. In addition to his mother's pride, the inventor won an international competition prize of $25,000 sponsored by Microsoft and a summer job installing his system at other restaurants.

The application has wider potential as well, for other operations such as hospitals, but it is dependent upon the Internet to work effectively.

Nothing Is Perfect

Let us assume you are willing and financially able to go further—that you are interested in a system to fit your planned operation. What should you do about it? In the past few pages I have painted a somewhat rosy picture of the advantages offered by a restaurant computer system. To begin, you must first examine what can go wrong. Your system is just as vulnerable a part of your operation as the chef who becomes ill, the power supply that fails, the dishwashing machine that breaks down, or the exhaust system that burns up. All these subsystems are much less likely to break down and interrupt the smooth running of your restaurant if they are periodically checked and serviced (yes, even the chef!). Someone must do preventive maintenance and replacement of worn parts and, unless you are unusual, it won't be you doing it.

Fortunately, computer programs cannot wear out. They *can* become obsolete, but more on that subject later.

Learn What Is Available

If you do not already have Internet access from a personal computer at home, go to the library to use one there and enter a few keywords into Google or another search engine. Key words such as "restaurant systems" or "cash registers" will get you started. If you are not familiar with doing such searches, one of the public library's wonderful research librarians will surely show you how to learn a lot in a short time. One of the many Web sites you find will likely have a local dealer or affiliate you can visit or invite to give you a presentation without obligation.

Local Service

Electronic and mechanical parts that comprise restaurant systems are subject to failure, especially printers. Sometimes they wear out. More often they are affected by mishandling or power fluctuations. These ills are preventable with proper electrical safeguards and good training of the staff. Although the number of moving parts is surprisingly small, even microelectronic elements occasionally need replacement. Just as you do for your dishwashing machine, you will have to depend on a local person or organization to fix your system.

The importance of having local service available at all times cannot be overemphasized. Your system will not wait to "crash" on a slow Monday. It will stop dead at 2:30 in the afternoon during Mother's Day dinner when your waiting room is so full, people are overflowing onto the sidewalk. Clearly, your system service must be available on all weekends and holidays.

Backup Capability

When the dishwashing machine breaks, you do your best to wash dishes well enough by hand to continue operations until the repair service arrives to fix it. Much the same will occur with your system, with one significant difference. People don't forget how to wash dishes by hand. Your dining room staff, however, will become so dependent on the system to do all I have heretofore mentioned that they may find it difficult to carry on without it. In a small restaurant it is easier than in a big one to drill the staff for such emergencies. You may wish to wait to install your system until you are sure you have a smooth operation without it. Or you can operate without the system at least one day per week for a month or so, until you are convinced that the staff can handle emergency operations manually.

Choosing a Dealer

When you are first considering which system to buy and from whom to buy it, prompt and reliable service should clearly be a top requirement. If you are located in a remote area, your chances of obtaining quick service are not great. But if you are anywhere in a major metropolitan area, you have an excellent chance of finding a dealer–service organization whose representative will be happy to discuss your particular case and suggest a system suitable for your restaurant.

Look for the qualities the sales representative exhibits as you make inquiries, listen to presentations, and read literature on various systems. The dealer who is already a well-established supplier will invite you to see systems in operation in restaurants. Spend the time it takes to observe and learn, and ask the same kinds of questions of the staff that I recommended you ask when viewing other restaurant kitchens (see chapter 2). It doesn't matter whether the restaurant is small or large.

A systems service organization may not limit its work to restaurants, since any number of retail businesses can use similar equipment with differing software. A new company may be just getting started in your area to provide the service you need. That shouldn't rule them out. The key to choosing your adviser is whether he or she has both restaurant experience and demonstrated knowledge of systems analysis. Ask to see resumes of those who purport to advise you. Honest, smart business-people may well give you a good deal because yours will be one of the places they'll show proudly to other potential customers.

How Much Is This Going to Cost?

Don't be surprised if the dealer wants to show you everything before discussing prices.

Prices Can Scare You Away

If you have not budgeted in your business plan for any system, then maybe you don't want one. If you do the work of becoming familiar with the systems available and decide that one will be a good asset, then revise your plan accordingly and shop for the best deal you can get within your budget. You should be able to buy a basic start-up system, including installation and training, for the amount you have realistically allocated. Consider, too, the prices for a cash register and the savings you'll realize through elimination of errors, and you may find that the system will pay for itself, so to speak, within a few years. So don't let a high-sounding price prevent you from investing the time needed to learn what's what.

If you already own a personal computer at home and have used a spreadsheet application or database software, you may find that you can get the management data you need directly from your accountant. By setting things up in advance, a weekly transfer of a few files will allow you to look at summary data or other financial indicators early in the morning or late at night, depending on your habit. Weekly and monthly reviews will help you make timely decisions for labor and supplies that will keep you profitable. It will also serve to keep your bookkeeper on schedule, knowing that you insist on seeing current data every week. Of course, you also need to consider whether your accountant would save time by getting the outputs from an in-house system and accordingly charge you much less.

Leasing

The suppliers of equipment for the restaurant industry take into account that their customers often start up with insufficient capital. For years, soft drink and beer suppliers have been leasing out equipment to ensure sales of their "consumables." The consumables in your system are repair and maintenance, and possible installation of equipment to modernize your system or expand its capability. By all means, explore terms for leasing a system with your supplier-dealer, but before you do, discuss the tax, legal, and insurance implications of such a lease with your accountant, attorney, and insurance agent. These discussions should help you formulate questions to ask the dealer when you negotiate the terms of the lease. Bear in mind that equipment manufacturers sell equipment.

If you don't buy a system, someone else has to before you can lease it. In times of high interest rates, the interest added to the lease price can make it less cost-effective to lease than to take advantage of tax reductions through cost recovery (depreciation) of owned equipment.

Used Systems

Judging from past trends in the small restaurant business, you may be offered a used system. But judging from trends in the computer business, it may be obsolete if it is more than six months old. Check the model names and numbers with the manufacturer to find out when it was first sold. Used equipment must be suited to your operation, not outdated, and still capable of providing years of satisfactory service. Be very cautious about such a system. Perhaps the dealer will be willing to sell it *and service it,* with a satisfactory guarantee, at a price that will make it worthwhile. But plan on spending money in the future to upgrade the system.

What Do You Get with Your System?

The dealer must ensure that you are adequately trained in the use of a system and that you can easily train your staff in its use. When being shown a system at a restaurant that has one, make sure to question the users about how long it takes to learn the system and to make periodic changes and adjustments.

It makes a lot of sense to have a touchscreen system. Not only do servers sometimes have wet fingers, but they also sometimes spill the liquids they are carrying. So the vulnerable keyboard that takes up counter space has become obsolete for restaurants.

Make sure you understand exactly how your system will accommodate changes—not just in prices, which may occur relatively often, but also when you want to add, delete, or modify items. For example, if your employees are assigned codes with which to identify themselves whenever they make an input, a list in the computer software must identify each code with an employee's name and, possibly, social security number. The system will refer to this table when it acts as a time clock and performs other functions that concern individual employees. Before you choose a system, you should fully understand exactly how this list of codes, and other such important and confidential system data, are safeguarded and modified when necessary.

Output Data

Your system should be capable of producing data files on a diskette or other media that are easily transferable to your accountant's system. Be sure to discuss this topic with both the dealer and your accountant to ensure that you do not have to pay for manual reentry of data for accounting and tax purposes.

Some systems print the time of day along with the date on guest checks. Make sure that the time-of-day feature can be suppressed, upon request, because some businesspeople would be embarrassed if the boss (or the spouse!) were to notice an odd time of day on a bar bill.

Printing

When your business records are kept in books and ledgers, it is simple to check on their current state; you just have to look at them. When dealing with electronically stored data, you must diligently label your diskettes with the date and contents. Otherwise, you run the risk of inadvertently destroying irreplaceable data, using out-of-date data, merging it irretrievably with composite records of business, and creating a mess of data the likes of which you would never be able to explain to the IRS auditor. A well-designed system will include a feature that identifies every stored file and prints out the identifying code along with the contents of the disk. But you must understand how this feature works and how it might be unintentionally bypassed. And you still must label the diskettes so that you don't waste time using the wrong one.

It is a good idea to have your accountant become familiar with your proposed system before you commit to installing it. He or she will be interested in the audit trails and features that will affect the business records needed for compliance with tax regulations and for other accounting purposes. Possibly, your accountant will find that a back-of-the-house program can reduce the number of work hours required for your monthly record keeping. He or she will at least make sure that the program is accurate and performs as advertised. If your accountant is not already familiar with restaurant systems, he or she should become so, or you should find an accountant who is.

There Are Less Expensive Ways

What I have described so far is a system capable of doing perhaps more than is really needed, and at too high a cost, for the owner of a small restaurant. A minimal system consists of only a register with a relatively simple input device and a connected guest check printer. With this type of system, two basic functions can be automated at a lower initial cost. The system has a microprocessor within the register and can have various options with costs and capabilities lying between those of the extremes described here. The computer chip advances of recent years and the low cost of memory have made such systems much more practical.

Eliminating Arithmetic Errors

The minimal setup will enable you to eliminate the errors servers often make when totaling the guest check. The register is capable of storing in its memory hundreds of different menu items, with prices for each. The server specifies the desired food or beverage by entering it in the input device. For the convenience of the servers, the menu is posted above the register with the proper number for each item clearly visible. After entering all items desired at the table during a particular course, the server pushes another button, which causes the register to produce a two-part order slip from a 2-inch-wide paper roll. On each half of the order slip is printed the name of each item (in abbreviated form) along with its price. The two halves are divided by a perforated line, with the date and the server's identification number on each. The microprocessor determines the price through a function called "price look up," often abbreviated to PLU in the trade. The same function is used to print the guest check.

Guest Check Printing

One of the best features of the expensive system previously described is often called the "retained check function." This enables the system to keep an internal record of all items ordered at a particular table, so that at the end of the meal the guest check can be printed at the press of a button. Because information in the memory is easily changed with this system, it is possible to void any errors and record changes in a customer's order so that the final guest check is uncluttered and clearly readable. With the simpler system, the server has more work to do each time another course is ordered. And the more entries the server must make, the greater the chance of making an error.

Controlling Flow of Orders

The two-part order slip provides a means of controlling how and when orders are sent to the kitchen or beverage area. The order slip pops up from the register and is automatically cut from the roll. The server writes on the slip the table number and any special instructions, such as cooking style or substitutions, and takes it to the kitchen or beverage dispenser. When items are delivered to the server, they are accompanied by half of the two-part slip. This is kept by the server for reconciliation at the end of the shift. The other half is retained by the kitchen or bartender for cross-checking against the server's shift total. The slips can also be used to update inventory.

For this system to work well, it is necessary for the server to have easy access to all her guest checks. If the server must carry them all in a pocket, it is too easy to hurriedly pull out and enter items on the wrong table's check. With this simple system, unfortunately, the only way to void an entry is to cross it off the check manually. Of course, the end-of-shift reconciliation must also void the amount involved. To avoid such errors, it's best to have a rack, labeled with each server's name, where checks can be slipped into slots (similar to a time-card rack near the punch clock). This takes up space and can be unsightly unless hidden from the dining room, but it makes it easier for the server to see the table number at the top of the guest check. It also makes it easy to arrange the checks in the order in which parties were seated or main courses were ordered. These manipulations make the server's job much more complicated than it would be with the retained check system.

Advantages and Drawbacks

The simpler system provides one of the main advantages of any system: It allows you to shift control of meal preparation sequencing from the kitchen to the server. It also eliminates the arithmetic errors that occur when employees have to look up prices or read sloppy handwriting. It offers the means for stricter control of what goes to the table; that is, if an item served isn't printed on the guest check, a discrepancy shows up between the total dollar value of items ordered by the server (an amount that is calculated automatically by the system) and the total of all the server's guest checks. This last total must be figured manually at the end of the shift, using the register as an adding machine. When a discrepancy cannot be accounted for by voided items, the source of the error must be found. Usually, the server is accountable for items omitted from the guest check. Such omissions are not possible with the retained check system, because the same actions that produce the order slip cause every price on it to be added to the stored totals for that table.

The main disadvantage of the simpler system is that it may lack significant back-of-the-house functions. At the end of the day, the manager can have printed out the percentage of total sales represented by each of the different categories of menu items. This is something, but not much. If the input device on the register is not versatile, the entry of new abbreviations for menu items becomes an exercise in ciphering.

The limited flexibility in the simpler system and its limited report capacity are the very characteristics that contribute to its lower price. The question for the small restaurant operator is whether the advantages that it offers, compared with either a completely manual operation or the more expensive system, are worth the cost. As the dealer is very likely to point out, if your alternative is a cash register, the simple system offers advantages that will soon pay for themselves.

Initial Cost Versus Life-of-the-System Cost

When your dealer shows you several restaurants with differing systems, be sure to ask the managers what additional costs besides the monthly service charge can be attributed to operating the system. Also, ask those managers who have had systems in operation for several years to give you some idea of how the annual costs have varied over time. The answers to these questions will help you assess which type of system you can afford. There are other considerations, too.

Price

When comparing systems, do not look only at the initial costs for hardware and software. Be sure to get a clear understanding of what these charges cover and how much the monthly service contract will cost, both before and after the manufacturer's warranty expires. Who pays for spare parts and for fixing software errors? Also, make sure you understand how the training for you and your staff will be paid for, and how many hours of training the price entitles you. You must learn to operate the system, but you must also make sure you can easily train others to do so. Because restaurant employees change jobs often, you cannot afford to rely on the dealer to train your new people. Make sure the system has a training mode, in which entries are just for practice and do not affect business data files. When visiting other restaurants, find an opportunity to ask members of the staff how long it took them to learn to use the system.

It is common for experienced servers to resist learning to use a new system. A waiter who worked for 30 years in a restaurant that used the simple system described here was adamant about not wanting to learn the new ways. Today, he is the one who is the most upset when the new system breaks down.

Try to get an idea of the likely cost of future improvements to the software or hardware for the system. If you want to take advantage of new developments or expanded capabilities offered by the manufacturer of the smaller system, you will very likely have to pay for them, especially if they involve any hardware adaptation. New software packages for the larger, more flexible systems, however, are more likely to be offered to you at little or no cost. With the simple system I've described, you may have the option of attaching a remote printer, which you could place in the kitchen. If you think this printer might be useful in the future, despite the fact that it will print neither table number nor special instructions (because these must be handwritten), make sure you get the basic register designed for easy connection to such a component. Otherwise, should you decide later to get a remote printer, you will have to pay for any electronic modifications needed.

Other Tradeoffs

Some differences between systems are not easily assessed just by comparing price. The time and energy spent by servers in movement to and from the kitchen is a hidden cost, especially in larger premises. In a small restaurant where servers already must go to the kitchen to grab salads, ladle soups, and assemble desserts, the trip to the kitchen to deliver an order slip may represent only a small percentage of the total transit time. However, small restaurants often have small kitchens, where any reduction of traffic will add to efficiency of operation. Thus, the system that substitutes the server's trip with the speed, accuracy, and convenience of an electronically transmitted message permits the servers to be assisted by a single kitchen helper, who prepares all items the cook does not and passes them to the servers. The key to efficiency here is that a few motions by the server at the touchscreen are translated into a permanent record and a usable printed order in the kitchen without requiring much movement in the work area. The time thus saved can be used to improve service at the table, which can increase the usage rate of tables—that is, improve "turnover"—if that is a goal for your place. Or it may allow three servers to do the work formerly done by four—a definite saving in labor cost. Or the servers may simply be less tired and friendlier. Such advantages are possible only if your system allows all necessary information to be entered at the touchscreen and automatically printed in the kitchen or beverage area.

Compare Service Costs, Too

When deciding between two levels of system capability, be sure to question the dealer closely about the differences in monthly service costs. Using the rule of thumb that system maintenance costs are about 10 percent of the purchase price per year, the less expensive system should be truly cheaper after 10 years of service than the higher priced system. But because the costs of maintenance and emergency repair service are based partly on the time needed to travel to your place of business and find the fault, the rule of thumb may not hold true in both cases. First, the travel time would be the same for either system and, second, the more expensive system may have built-in fault isolation and test capabilities that allow the repair to be completed in less time. So the prices for the two service contracts may be nearly equal. If this is the case, the difference in total cost between the two systems won't be nearly as great as would be indicated by simply comparing the initial purchase prices.

Keep in mind that the foregoing assumes you will not upgrade either system for 10 years. This assumption may prove to be a naïve one in today's world of technological advances.

Should You Be Online?

If you decide to install a restaurant system, it will most likely be a stand-alone operation within your premises and may or may not have the ability to connect to the Internet. You will have to decide what value you may derive, if any, from such added capability that can be had separately from a PC and a connection to an Internet service provider (ISP). Remember that a stand-alone system cannot be attacked by a virus or by a hacker if it is never connected to the outside world.

The WWW and E-Commerce

The World Wide Web and its link to almost every topic or organization that can be of use to you does not require you to install a restaurant system. You can do it from home or the library. What does the Web offer you to enhance your business? I have already mentioned the need to surf the Web sites of those who supply restaurant equipment and automated systems. You may also do the same to find produce, meat, and staples suppliers even before their sales representatives descend upon you. E-mail offers you a way to be in daily or weekly contact with your suppliers, even in the middle of the night or on weekends when offices are closed. You are not limited to local contacts or time zone constraints when using such channels. You may have luck in getting a good deal on insurance by searching the Web for your needs. If you are comfortable with buying online, you may be able to find items of interest for your restaurant décor or specialty displays that are offered via online auctions or by faraway dealers.

Your Own Web Site

The biggest decision you will face related to the Web is whether you want to have your own Web site. You do not have to know much about how to create one in order to do so, but you will have to select and register a Web address that no one else has, so it could influence what name you choose for your restaurant. The address comprises two parts after the initial "www." The first part is called the domain name, which is followed by a dot. The domain name cannot use certain punctuation marks. The second portion is called the suffix and for a commercial entity is either "com" or "biz." For example, if you are thinking of naming your restaurant Matilda's Waltz, with décor reminiscent of Australia, you must make sure that the domain name MatildasWaltz.com or .biz is not already taken. If it is, and it is not associated with food service, you can try "MatildasWaltzRestaurant.com." If someone has already opened a place with the name you need and the matching domain name, but it is far away from your location, you can modify the basic name by adding your town name or street name to obtain a unique domain name. Call 800-880-8208 to register your domain name and ask about naming restrictions.

Web Site Offerings

You can think of a Web site as an ad on the biggest advertising medium in the world. It offers you the means for displaying, in full color and with the simplest or most sophisticated artistry or photography, what you offer to the public, who you are, and why people should come to taste your culinary wares. It does not have to change much, if at all, once it is created. If you have a PC at home with e-mail connectivity through an ISP, you will find that your ISP can host your business Web site by providing an amount of space on its Internet server for which you are charged a modest fee each month. The space you use will be determined by how many pages you wish to display and how complex you wish to make the story being shown to the public. How much can a small restaurant say, beyond the basics? That can be influenced by such events as your presenting live musical performers each week or periodically, for which you need to update your Web site to draw in their fans. But you can also simply inform Web surfers that you do present such performances and that they should call for information. The basic display does not have to change unless something shown is no longer correct.

Web Site Design

An ISP such as Earthlink can offer you referrals to Web designers as well as an easy-to-use tool to discover whether your proposed domain name is already taken. Almost anywhere in the country these days, you can find the services of a graphic artist who is also a specialist in creating both art and advertising for the Web. Many have done so for small restaurants. One of the best ways to find one locally, besides simply consulting the phone book, is to look at other restaurant Web sites in your region. If you see one that particularly impresses you, a call to the restaurant manager should result in your getting the name of the creative talent.

If that is not satisfactory, or if it results in too much cost, try making contact with a local community college art or computer science department. There is probably a student or perhaps an instructor who would love to design your site, though you may get less than what a seasoned professional would provide.

Whomever you get to build your Web site, make sure it is written so that you are able to make necessary changes in the future and you have control of the file in the form of a backup copy. That will allow you to have someone else make future corrections and changes, even if your original designer is no longer available. If the designer makes the arrangement for your Web address by registering it in your name, make sure you know all the details of how long the address is valid for and how often it needs to be renewed. Renewal should be your responsibility, and you need to pay the annual fee in a timely manner to the company that maintains the Web address.

13

What to Do If . . .

PREPARE YOURSELF for the unexpected, the unusual, and the worst. Find the nearest emergency hospital and the most competent medical practitioners in your area. (They are probably among your patrons, if you have a fine dinner reputation.) Post a telephone list where it will be most readily used to call an ambulance, the fire department, the police or sheriff, and the rescue squad. Make connection with a competent attorney. Place your insurance with a local firm that can serve you in person rather than by phone or mail, and add the agent's number to your emergency telephone list.

Anticipate building emergencies. Keep handy the telephone number of the person who services your automatic fire extinguisher system. Find a reliable electrician and plumber who will provide emergency service on weekends, and have them inspect your building to become familiar with the layout. You may need the services of the person who operates a sewer-pipe reaming device. Locate and mark all the available waste pipe clean-out fixtures. When a sewer line clogs or your exhaust fan motor burns out in the middle of a busy Saturday night, you must have someone available who will not tell you to wait until Monday morning.

People Emergencies

People emergencies are inevitable. Eventually, someone will become ill or be injured in your restaurant. Someone will fall down the stairs or trip over a loose spot in the carpet. An employee will cut himself on a sharp knife or piece of glass. In dealing with these events, you have only to follow a few simple rules:

- Remain calm and speak in a low, even voice.

- Give specific directions to people who can assist.

- In serious cases, call the rescue squad at once.

- Perform first aid competently, and notify a doctor.

If possible, move the injured person out of the dining room into an area where he or she can be isolated from the public. It is best, however, not to move a person who may be seriously injured. In such cases, first aid and comfort should be administered without regard for unavoidable onlookers. In a small restaurant, medically trained people present will usually identify themselves and offer to assist. You should know the proper first aid for choking, burns, severe bleeding, coronary episodes, and other common acute medical emergencies.

Everyone who works in a restaurant should know how to perform first aid for choking victims. The cardiopulmonary resuscitation (CPR) procedure that employs the chest thrust or abdominal thrust to dislodge an object in the airway of a conscious person is taught by qualified CPR instructors, and you should take a local class. Special precautions are required for children and pregnant women. Choking is one of the three most common causes of accidental death in the United States; when people drink alcoholic beverages, eat meat, and talk too much, the danger of choking increases. In California restaurants, a poster describing the procedures must be displayed where employees can study it. You should try to arrange for a paramedic or other qualified person to demonstrate CPR and first aid for obstruction of the air passage to you and your staff. Recent data indicate that chest depression along with a clear air passage probably provides enough lung compression to obviate the need for mouth-to-mouth breathing. A plastic device to prevent contact with the person's body fluids may be recommended by the instructor.

If a foreign object or substance is accidentally present in food served to a customer, you should know what to do. Someone may break a tooth on an inexplicable piece of gravel or cut his tongue on a piece of glass. Your liability insurance for "completed operations" will cover these cases. Instruct your servers to take the injured person immediately to the restroom or kitchen and to call you. Sometimes hysteria will result from such unfortunate occurrences, and you should know how to calm down and treat the person. Once the person has been given proper treatment, it is time to make a record of the date and time of the incident, the names of witnesses, and other pertinent facts for your insurance report. Make no contentions regarding negligence. Simply record what happened as best you can and promise to report it to the proper agency. Do not argue with anyone, especially within the dining area. Let an air of calm assurance prevail, even if you are very upset.

Make sure your kitchen first-aid supplies are kept current. If an employee is injured, you should be able to provide adequate treatment and protection for a minor wound. Burns should be kept under ice water for at least five minutes. For anything more serious, such as a bad burn or a cut that might require stitches or that will not stop bleeding, you should insist that the injury be examined by a doctor or that the employee go to the emergency room of a hospital immediately. Many employees will not want to do that, but it is necessary for your own protection in case of later infection or complications. Your workers' compensation insurance will cover the cost of medical treatment, and state laws require that such injuries be reported.

Food Safety

Allergic reactions to certain foods such as nuts require you to indicate on the menu description that an entrée is prepared with such items. If the nut or other allergenic ingredient is not obvious in your secret recipe, you should at least remind the at-risk patron to ask the server about ingredients by inviting such questions with a notice posted on the wall or listed on the menu.

The likelihood that your kitchen or wait staff will be the source of a virus or other disease organism transmitted to the public remains low, despite the conditions reported in cases of SARS, or Asian Flu. This assumes that you are aware of and practice proper food storage, refrigeration, cooking, and food handling procedures. Nevertheless, you should be especially vigilant during the seasons for such ailments to ensure that your servers are not sick and transmitting a virus. Encourage them to request that a substitute be called in for their shift and reward them for doing so in whatever way you can. If you have items on your menu that are particularly perishable or known to carry risks, such as mussels and other live shellfish, become an expert on what can go wrong and act accordingly.

If you are a professionally trained chef, you have probably studied the array of animal and plant organisms that can cause disease or toxic reactions. And you know how to analyze your menu items prudently to defend your work from such threats. If you follow all the rules for keeping food at the proper temperature, using reliable suppliers, and discarding out-of-date items, you will have no problems. The study and prevention process known as Hazard Analysis and Critical Control Points is commonly referred to as HACCP. If you are not professionally trained, a HACCP course is well worth your time.

To whet your curiosity for the subject, I provide below a partial description of some of the organisms and substances that you will encounter in your study. Bacteria, molds, and yeasts fall into a group of unicellular microorganisms, while viruses are not even living cells in the strictest sense. The viruses associated with food include Hepatitis A and the Norwalk gastrointestinal virus. Most foodborne illness is caused by bacteria, but the bacteria that spoil food do not typically cause illness in someone who eats the spoiled food. So-called "food poisoning" usually results from the release of a toxin by bacteria that have contaminated the food, or the contaminated food is the carrier of bacteria that sickens people. *Clostridium botulinum* and *Staphylococcus aureus* are examples of the former; *Escherichia coli, Salmonella,* and *Vibrio parahaemolyticus* are examples of the latter, which can grow in food. Other bacteria that cause dysentery, tuberculosis, and cholera do not grow in, but can be carried by, food. Learning more about the condition caused by *C. botulinum,* known as botulism, is a sufficiently good reason to take a course in food safety.

Food yeasts are not pathogenic but can cause spoilage. Molds, which are classed as a type of fungi, can be pathogenic. Those that are produce a mycotoxin. One of the more common mycotoxins, aflatoxin, is a known carcinogen.

In your study, you will learn that the onset of food poisoning symptoms varies from hours to days, depending on the cause. For the longer incubation or intoxication periods, the victim may feel quite well and may visit a restaurant. The important points to remember for the restaurant owner are that simply because a person becomes ill after eating at a restaurant does not mean that the source of the illness is to be found there or in the food consumed there. Only a test of the food and the premises, compared with the presence of the same pathogen in the intestine of the victim, can lead to such a conclusion.

The probability that someone will be made ill by eating at a restaurant has most likely not increased as the result of contaminated water or new strains of resistant microorganisms. If the odds have gotten worse, it is because people are eating as many as 60 percent of their meals away from home or prepared outside the home.

Building Emergencies

Fires are preventable. Invite the local fire inspector to check out your premises each year. He may save you a lot of grief. But if a grease fire does occur, even if you have an automatic fire extinguisher system or sprinklers, you should try to put it out with a large hand-held carbon-dioxide extinguisher kept in the kitchen. The carbon-dioxide extinguisher offers the advantage that it does not harm food that is sprayed with it. Most of the automatic systems, in contrast, have two disabling effects on your kitchen. First, they cover everything with a fine chemical dust that is inedible, so the food must be discarded. Second, they automatically trip a valve that shuts off the gas supply to the kitchen. Before you can cook again, the valve must be reset by your fire-extinguisher serviceperson.

If a fire does set off the automatic system, you will probably have to shut down for the night, or suffer at least a several-hour delay. If your fire-extinguisher service person is available immediately, and not too much food was ruined, you may be able to get going again after the gas-line valve is reset, which takes a short time. Discuss the procedure with the service person when he installs your system.

If you should have a dining room fire, or if someone ignites his clothing or your curtains, try to put it out with a hand-held extinguisher of the proper type, which should be kept in or near the dining room. Your carpeting and drapes should be resistant to flame, but your linens will not be. It is imperative that all ashtrays be dumped into a container not used for paper or dirty linens. Many kitchen fires result from sloppy handling of ashtrays that still contain embers.

When an electrical failure cuts off power to your building, you should be ready to continue as best you can under other types of artificial light, such as battery lights, camping lanterns, candles, or kerosene lamps. Many jurisdictions require emergency lights in the dining room and kitchen to allow safe departure by the public and the employees during a power failure. If the interruption of power is within your building and you cannot solve it by resetting the circuit breaker, you must get your electrician to come right away. The same is true for plumbing trouble.

Robbery and Burglary

Discuss the subject of armed robbery with your local police. If you have any large amount of cash on hand on a weekend, you could be a target, especially if you are in or near a high-crime area. Ask how best to protect the lives and property of your customers, your employees, and yourself. Then issue instructions to those who regularly or occasionally operate the cash register. Become familiar also with the methods used by quick-change artists, who usually try to work their scam on young employees who have to make change at the cash register. You and your staff should also learn how to recognize counterfeit money.

If you discover significant amounts of food, supplies, or equipment missing, whether or not there is evidence of a break-in, report the facts to the police. If food and supplies are disappearing, take a close look at the methods you use for issuing supplies from storage and for controlling access to locked areas. Hold a staff meeting to discuss the problem, and ask for suggestions from your employees on what to do. If you suspect that the culprits are local people, or even friends of your employees, work with the police burglary expert to apprehend them.

Business Slump

If you are keeping close track of your business, you will know when you are beginning to get into financial trouble. Do not wait for your accountant to tell you the bad news. Respond to a temporary loss of business by immediately reducing your labor costs as much as possible and by really cutting down on waste. Prepare to offer and advertise some good specials if the slump continues. Make some small but noticeable changes in your dining room or in front of your building. Even a fresh coat of paint or some new attraction in the front windows will cause people to take notice and want to see what is going on inside. Consider bringing in some special entertainment on certain nights. If times are hard, the cost may be lower than you think, and you can always offer to pay in part with food.

If the slump persists, you should consider getting a professional analysis of your operation and of the problems you are having. If your primary food supplier salesperson has owned or operated a restaurant, he or she may be a good source of suggestions. The Small Business Administration (SBA) can offer some advice. There are also volunteer organizations of retired businesspeople who remain active by helping other small and medium-size businesses succeed. The local SBA office should be able to direct you to one of these groups. This kind of counseling is available at little or no cost and can provide invaluable advice and encouragement to help you turn things around. All of these steps should be taken while you are still operating in the black or close to the break-even level.

Big Trouble

Even after taking over as much of the work as you and your partner can handle yourselves, and after determining that your prices and portions are right and no one is stealing your food, you may not have enough business to turn a profit after expenses. You have a hard choice to make: relocate, try to sell the business, or cease operations. The real reasons for your restaurant's failure may be very basic: reputation, the limitations of your overall menu and dining room design, or some other problem too big to correct.

Relocation

It rarely makes sense to relocate when you are in business trouble. An exception might be if you have the chance to get a nicer place in a more convenient spot, perhaps even at the same or lower cost, or the chance to buy rather than rent a building. Your long-term lease arrangement may discourage you from making a move at all under your existing business name. But if you are close enough to your old location for your name to be worth transferring to the new one, you will merely be moving your troubles to a different spot. If an independent analysis shows that in fact you could do better at another, available location, however, and your operation is basically sound, the trouble of moving might just be worth it. It will not be easy.

Selling Out

Even if you decide to move, you might consider selling your equipment and the lease to someone else who wants to try to make a go of your present location. If you plan to relocate your business, you should retain the right to your name, of course, and you should not sign any noncompetition agreement that would prevent you from opening at the new location. Or, if you are retiring from the restaurant business, you can sell your name as well.

When you look back on it all, don't cry . . . smile.

List your business with a reputable broker, who will tell you what you are likely to net from a sale. You may have to set a much lower asking price than you would like, especially if all you have to sell is your equipment, your leasehold, and a business that is barely making a profit. However, during hard times there are often people who feel shaky about their positions in industry and who have some small savings that they think it wise to invest in a small business. One may come along who believes he can do better than you did.

Closing

If you have allowed the business to dwindle in value to the point where no one is willing to buy it, then you have essentially a worthless business and some valuable equipment. Your lease may be worth something, depending on whether someone could pay the rent by operating a different kind of business in the building.

You will want to get as much for your equipment as possible. If you are not in or near a major city, you may have to call in a used-equipment dealer or auctioneer to offer you whatever he thinks it is worth. Get bids on the whole set of equipment from as many dealers as you can. If you are in a city, you may find it better to advertise the equipment yourself and to try to sell the larger items without having to pay any commission. There is some advantage, though, to having everything sold in one day. Therefore, it may be best for you to hold an auction right on your premises conducted by one of the reputable auctioneers in the area. Make sure it is advertised well and held on a good day for local restaurant people. If you are in a small town, it may be best for you to hire someone to haul your equipment to the nearest large city that has restaurant auctions and dealers. Do not hurt your back moving anything. You will be especially vulnerable to such injuries as you see your pride and (former) joy dispersed. You should also confer very closely with your accountant and attorney about what steps to take to protect yourself from claims that could hold up the sale. They can explain to you the advantages and disadvantages of voluntary bankruptcy proceedings.

On that somber note I conclude this book, adding only these few final observations. Nothing is forever. You may create the finest small restaurant in the state. It may give you the greatest feeling of accomplishment and security you have ever known, despite the incredible amount of hard labor and devotion it demands. But someday you will find that it is time to change the locks on your security, or someone will try to take it all away from you. You may lose a negligence suit over something that was not your fault. There are no guarantees in the restaurant business, or in life. The only true security is in doing your best at whatever you choose to do. The real adventure is always a risk. To say, "I once thought about opening a restaurant," doesn't count. Are you alive? Then go on, open your little restaurant.

Index

Children
  irritable, handling, 129
  of restaurant owners, 3–4, 29
  seating for, 76, 80
Choking victims, 230
Cleanup
  crew members, 112–13
  daily chores, 171–73, 175
  periodic chores, 173–76, 175
  in restrooms, 177–78
  "side work," 176
  weekly chores, 175
Closing down restaurant, 236–37
Coats, safekeeping of, 117
Codes, building, 84
Codes, food service, 31
Codes, health, 60
Coffee, serving, 196
Coffeepots, 77
Community theater, 188–89
Compact disks (CDs), 87, 89–90
Completion bonds, 24
Computers. *See also* Restaurant com-
    puter systems
  designing menu on, 50
  in office, 68
  podcasting and, 187
Concrete floors, 57, 172
Contractors, 37
Contracts, employment, 163
Cooling devices, 79
Counter service, 74–75
Credit cards, 82, 131
Culinary schools, 10, 161–62
Customers. *See* Guests

Décor, 34–35, 78–81, 85
Deed restrictions, 25
Deep-fat fryers, 56
Deliveries, overnight, 142
Delivery people, 143
Desserts
  complimentary, 124, 126
  selection of, 124
  taking orders for, 110, 124–25
Dining room(s)
  capacity, 36
  cashier station in, 81–84
  cleaning, 112
  décor, 78–81
  dinner theater in, 91–92
  floors, cleaning, 176–77
  furnishings for, 71–78
  live performers for, 90–91

music for, 87–90
"no-noes," 129
windows in, 39
Dinner prices, 191–95
Dinner theater, 91–92
Discount affiliations, 193–95
Diseases, 231–33
Dishwasher duties, 113, 166–67
Dishwashing machines
  alternatives to, 174
  cleaning, 173
  equipment, about, 65–67
  supply service for, 143–45
Door locks, 36, 86, 205
Doors, swinging, 60–61
Drink orders
  in restaurant "system," 209–11, 220–21
  server's handling of, 108, 119, 120
Drug use, 169
Dust, removing, 176

Electrical service, 37–38, 234
Emergencies
  building-related, 229, 233–34
  financial, 234–37
  medical, 229–33
  robbery and burglary, 234
Employees. *See also specific types*
  alcoholic consumption by, 165
  application cards, 154–56
  birthdays, acknowledging, 154
  in business plan, 16, 17
  dismissing, 168–69
  disqualifying traits, 157
  fringe benefits for, 204–5
  hiring, 17, 153–63
  immigrant, 167
  interaction among, analysis of,
      58–61
  language used by, 105, 133–35
  managing, 6, 153
  meals for, 165–66, 204–5
  meetings for, 165
  panic among, avoiding, 10
  parking for, 37, 189
  part-time, 167–68
  personal belongings, 68–69
  personnel records, 154, 157–58
  physical stress on, 10
  scheduling, 167–68
  summer resort labor, 169–70
  teamwork among, 10
  theft by, 205
  training, 17, 164–67

About the Author

Daniel Miller co-founded the Grey Fox Inn, a successful small restaurant in Cambria, California. After a varied career spanning such industries as cutlery sales, beer brewing, newspaper advertising, and computer systems analysis and procurement, he is now semi-retired and lives in Reston, Virginia.

A Note to Seminar Leaders and Educators

If you'd like to use this book in your classroom, you or your organization can purchase copies at a significant discount directly from The Harvard Common Press. A minimum order of 12 copies is required. For more details, or to place an order, contact us at 617-423-5803 or e-mail orders@harvardcommonpress.com.